Loughrea

A PARISH HISTORY

Loughrea

A PARISH HISTORY

DECLAN KELLY

The
History
Press
Ireland

For Bertie

First published 2014

The History Press Ireland
50 City Quay
Dublin 2
Ireland
www.thehistorypress.ie

© Declan Kelly, 2014

The right of Declan Kelly to be identified as the Author
of this work has been asserted in accordance with the
Copyright, Designs and Patents Act 1988.

British Library Cataloguing in Publication Data.
A catalogue record for this book is available from the British Library.

ISBN 978 1 84588 827 5

Typesetting and origination by The History Press

CONTENTS

FOREWORD

The writing of a local history is a very important undertaking as it records for posterity the story of a people and their place, making it available and accessible to present and future generations to appreciate and enjoy. It is very often the case that written history can be at odds with locally held 'truths'.

In this account of the eight parishes that make up the Catholic Deanery of Loughrea, the author, Declan Kelly, has taken an interesting approach. Instead of looking at the hard facts of history as a basis for his work, he has instead tapped into an alternative source of material comprising of a rich vein of oral history and local folk memory to relay the popular history of the region. A mix of folklore and storytelling, this book relates the stories of the clergy, their parishioners and a myriad of others that relate in some way to the everyday life of a rural Irish parish. It does not pretend to be a heavy academic study, but instead is a wonderful weaving of the tales and beliefs and indeed misplaced beliefs of a traditional society. It describes a people who while steadfast in their Catholic faith also clung on to a parallel world of superstition and folk tradition, much of which permeated their lives.

In this book the supernatural is never too far from the minds of the people. Clergy are given miraculous powers, while certain places in the landscape are imbued with a sense of the supernatural and are spoken about and treated with both fear and respect. Ghosts and fairies, the banshee, strange happenings that could only be understood in a supernatural sense were all part of everyday life. What comes out in this book is a deep respect for people and life and an acceptance of death celebrated by popular folk ritual.

Living in what we now believe to be a more enlightened era we tend to dismiss the traditions and beliefs of the recent past as simple and naïve. However, we should not forget that for those whose memories are recounted here this was the stuff of everyday life. It was real to them and therefore vital to our own understanding of who we are.

Dr Christy Cunniffe

INTRODUCTION

The writing of a book is not unlike the making of soup. One chops so much of one ingredient here and slices so much of another there, until the right mix is achieved. Of course, in making soup, one doesn't empty all the edible contents of one's larder into the pot and so a sense of culinary discrimination is advised. The writer hopes that his literary prowess exceed his skills in the kitchen.

When compiling an official history of the diocese of Clonfert some years ago, the writer found that after the work had been assembled, a goodly amount of material was left over. This was mostly folklore and though undoubtedly invaluable, it could not be incorporated into the text without giving the reader literary indigestion. Thus, the idea for a work of this nature grew, lest it be lost. The material is all the more remarkable when one considers that it was gathered in 1931 by an t-Athair Eric McFhinn, a noted polyglot and scholar of the diocese. An t-Athair Eric carried off this not inconsiderable task by circulating *cóipleabhair* to colleagues around the diocese and asking them to follow a set schema for recording the folklore and history of their respective parishes. Taken in conjunction with the Schools Folklore Commission's work a few years later, this material now has a value beyond even that which was foreseen at the time. As there is always a law of diminishing returns with local historical knowledge, one suspects there may be some duplication.

It is moderately surprising that no attempt has been made in recent years to emulate the work of the Commission on a nationwide level. One might suggest that it would be of particular value in recording experiences of the Second World War and of the customs and emotions surrounding emigration. Moreover, it would introduce a new generation to the study of the local past via a rigorous scheme of enquiry. The *Schema and Questionnaire for Parish Histories* which an t-Athair Eric published in 1929 would certainly stand the test of time were it to be revisited. It would be encouraging if the current focus on the Gathering were to act as a catalyst for such a programme. It would be momentous if it were to raise the question of bringing home not only those who have ready cash to spend, but also those who left this country to build other countries and have now fallen on hard and lonely times.

Shortly after being appointed archivist to Clonfert diocese, the writer discovered that the late Revd Dr Kevin Egan had spent 1941–1945 following his then bishop, Dr John Dignan, about the diocese and photographing occasions of importance. It was quite an achievement at the time and is a tribute to Kevin's dedication. Petrol had been rationed, photographic apparati was in scant supply and he was obliged to set up a darkroom in his rooms at the Presbytery in Ballinasloe. He had already been helping an t-Athair Eric from 1938, at Dr Dignan's request, in researching the history of the diocese. As little or no funding was available for developing the photographs, the current writer dug into his own slender resources and developed them over the course of three years. Revd Dr Egan believed they would be 'of interest' in years to come. His words were characteristically modest as this work recorded images of all the churches (some of which have been long since demolished) and of the interiors which bid fair to have rivalled the more decorative of those on the Continent. Some may reflect, when looking upon them, that the reorderings that swam in the wake of the Second Council did not always do justice to the richness of our Christian heritage. These images also capture a way of life which has long since vanished and show a remarkably resilient spirit among a people suffering the privations of the Emergency years. Unfortunately, the confirmandi and their teachers are not named, though dates are given where indicated. A perusal of the relevant parochial register of confirmations for that year should ascertain if a close relative is indeed depicted.

In June of 1922, in a singularly unhelpful exercise, some doughty Irishmen set off a landmine in the Public Records Office of the Four Courts. Thousands of old documents were destroyed, including the remaining censi from the nineteenth century and many of the Church of Ireland registers. The country was in the vice-grip of the Civil War and, alas, everything was grist to the military mill. Happily, just before this happened, one Thomas T. O'Farrell had taken the time to type out extracts from the censi taken in

Loughrea in 1821 and 1841 and they are reproduced here in print for the first time. These now have a huge value and we must give thanks to the Heavens for the late Professor O'Farrell's commitment to researching aspects of a town with which he had familial links. For those seeking to research family links, the best genealogical organisation the writer has encountered is the East Galway Family History Society in Woodford, County Galway.

A deep debt of gratitude is due to Pat Barrett, a native of Loughrea, who was ever-available to give advice. One cannot sit for long in Pat and Marie Barrett's company without eagerly subscribing to the happy belief that 'God is in His Heaven and all is well'. Pat generously gave the current writer unlimited access to both his time and his extensive photographic collection and rightly enjoys the reputation for being one of the foremost authorities on the history of Loughrea. His memorably titled *The Ten Commandments, the Revival of Irish and a Kick in the Arse*, is *de rigueur* for anyone who seeks an honest and entertaining book about Loughrea's history and folklore. I am especially grateful for the notes he provided from Sr Francis Fahey on the old Pro-cathedral of St Brigid. Thanks are also due to Dr Christy Cunniffe who agreed at alarmingly short notice to supply a foreword for the present work and whose own indefatigable investigations of the fields and hedgerows of south-east Galway have saved many a forgotten monument from an uncertain fate. If he has missed an archaeological feature in any of the parishes he has trawled, it must be as well hidden as the Lost City of Atlantis. Dr Brian Casey has recently filled the role of archivist to Clonfert diocese and I am grateful to him for proofreading the manuscript and offering many helpful suggestions. I am especially grateful to Most Revd John Kirby, Bishop of Clonfert, for his permission to use material from the archives of Clonfert diocese and to Senator Lorraine Higgins who is one of the few public representatives the current writer has met who seems interested in the heritage of south-east Galway and who encouraged the writer to see the work through its various stages.

Thanks are also due to natives of the various parishes and others who filled in the gaps or gave valuable assistance through the years, such as Mrs Angela Bane, Ms Geraldine Bane, Mr Oliver Barrett, Mr Fergus Benson, Mr J.J. Broderick, Mr Brendan Burke, Ms Kathleen Callanan, Mr Sean and Mrs Eileen Callanan, Mr Sean Cleary, Ms Mary Coen, Mrs Mary Jo Costello, Mr Johnny Cowan, Mr Steven Dolan, Mr Pakie Dolphin, Mr Gerry Donnellan, Mr Bertie Donohoe (RIP), Mr Michael Donohoe, the family of the late Fr Pascal Donohoe, Mr Dermot and Mrs Angela Donohue, Mr Hugh Joe Fahy, Mr Jim Fahy, Mr Martin Fahy, Ms Eleanor Flynn, Mrs Mary Finnerty,

Mr Jack Forde, Mr Joe Glynn, Mr Theo Hanley, Mrs Ciss Hardiman (RIP), Mr Eamon Hayes, Red Phil Hearty, Mrs Geraldine Hodgins, Cllr Pat Hynes, Mrs Mary Kilkenny, Mr Barry Lally, Mr Paddy Larkin, Revd Brendan Lawless, Mr Jimmy Leahy, Mrs Ciss Lyons, Mrs Marie Lyons, Senator Michael Mullins, Mrs Marie O'Carra, Mr Sean and Mrs Lillian O'Dwyer, Mr Séamus Ó Grádaigh, Mr John Joe O'Malley (RIP), Mr Colman O'Shaughnessy, Mr Paraig and Mrs Bridie Pender, Mr John Joe Rabbitte, Mrs May Roche, Mrs Eileen Sheehy, Cmdt Fiona Smith, Mrs Teresa Smyth, Mr Pat and Mrs Mary Smyth, Msgr Ned Stankard, Mrs Joan Treacy, Mr Tom Treacy and Mrs Eithne Whiriskey. My sincere thanks also to the editorial staff of The History Press for their courtesy and professionalism, particularly Beth Amphlett.

The material included in this volume comes from a variety of sources, mostly the archives of the diocese of Clonfert and from my own personal archive, built up over ten years of gathering items of interest. As such, it is something of a curate's egg though it is hoped that all who read it will find something different of interest. Wherever feasible, sources are cited in the text. A number of items come from having interviewed elderly parishioners over the space of a decade. Many are now gone to their eternal rest and they well deserve a peaceful slumber, for it was often their kind words and old-world decency that gave a weary heart a welcome boost. Many now consent to the belief that the world we live in has become a strange and hostile place and that the milk of human kindness has all but curdled in every town in Ireland. If that perception is ever to be arrested and reversed, it will only be through reinventing simple values like compassion, honour and basic manners.

We now know that the past was not often as innocent as it seemed at the time and that the full measure of truth behind the well-worn epithet 'the good old days' is open to debate. Not a day seems to pass without some public figure being wheeled out onto national television to give an account of the stewardship of their own professional bailiwick and that is not a bad thing. The past in Ireland was often a place where people viewed reality through a glass darkly and where obeisance to authority figures was automatically granted rather than earned. Thus, the potential for the abuse of authority was all too high. There are many stories of the missioner preaching from the pulpit in declamatory tones as his listeners quaked in their boots. Yet, there are also many stories of acts of great kindness and compassion by parish clergy, to the extent that the graves of some are the final point of pilgrimage for locals to this day. We cannot deny that a substantial number who negotiated those decades were honest and honourable and lived their lives in the best way they knew how.

The parishes dealt with in this volume are Mullagh/Killoran, Loughrea, Leitrim/Kilmeen, Kiltullagh/Killimordaly/Attymon, Cappatagle/Kilrickle, Carrabane, New Inn/Bullaun and Killeenadeema/Aille. Alas, photographic images were plentiful in some instances and not so plentiful in others. To those who may feel slighted, *mea culpa*; the objective was honourable. This volume is the flagship for two more, which treat of the parishes clustering Ballinasloe and then Portumna. It is envisaged that a complete episcopal succession and all references to Clonfert diocese in valuable historical documents such as the *Papal Regesta* will be included in a future volume. Each parish of the diocese has made a contribution to vocations to the priesthood and religious life and while it is only possible to mention a few in the constraints of the current volume, it is envisaged that a future volume will contain as comprehensive a list as can be produced for all parishes. The writer's primary aspiration, however, is that these books will not only evoke good memories of a time that now seems almost impossible to imagine but that it will inspire others to put pen to paper to record further aspects of the finite resource that is our heritage.

The late Bertie Donohoe was a good friend and a sound advisor. Much that the current writer learned about the history of Loughrea, and indeed Clonfert diocese, was learned from him. At his funeral, the late Archbishop Joseph Cassidy captured something of the essence of Bertie when he said:

> He was the most wonderful storyteller I ever came across ... He didn't just recall the past. He recreated it. He made it happen again before your eyes ... he had a knowledge of the town and its environs that nobody else could match.

Thus, this book is dedicated to his memory.

One of nature's gentlemen and dapper to the last ... Bertie Donohoe who wrote for the
Connacht Tribune under the pen-name 'JBD'. (Courtesy of Oliver Barrett)

GLOSSARY

Given that the Church is some 2,000 years old, it has naturally acquired considerable ritual encrustation. That the concomitant terminology is not altogether self-explanatory was illustrated a number of years ago after the writer was innocently asked when visiting a house, 'And how long have you been canonised now?' To assist those of all creeds and none with understanding the more arcane ecclesiastical terms and abbreviations, the following glossary is included. Some secular abbreviations are also included.

CA   Catholic Administrator, sometimes also styled *Adm.*

CC   Catholic Curate.

Chancellor   The official responsible for a diocesan chancery through which official correspondence and documentation passes.

CM   Congregation of the Mission. Members are referred to as Vincentians.

Coadjutor   From Latin *coadiuvare*/to help. The coadjutor is a bishop who assists the bishop-proper and has right of succession. The late Archbishop Joseph Cassidy was once asked the difference between an auxiliary bishop and a coadjutor. His reply is worth repeating. 'An auxiliary bishop usually greets the bishop of the diocese with the question "How can I help you this morning my Lord?" The coadjutor bishop usually greets the bishop with the question "How are you feeling this morning, my Lord?"'

Confirmation	A sacrament bestowed on a baptised person by which they receive the Holy Spirit and are emboldened in grace. As it was understood at the time many of the images in this book were recorded, confirmation was the sealing of a person as a soldier of Christ. Confirmandi were anointed on the foreheads with the oil of chrism and gently struck or tapped on the cheek by the bishop who recited the words 'Peace be with thee'. The tap to the cheek was symbolic of the difficulties that the candidate would endure in the Christian life.
Deanery	A group of parishes within a diocese.
Deconsecration	There is no formal ritual for the deconsecration of a church-building, though churches appear to lose their consecrated status once events of a sacred character cease to occur within. The Code of Canon Law covers this under Canon 1212 which states: 'Sacred places lose their dedication or blessing if they suffer major destruction or if they have been permanently given over to profane uses, de facto or through a decree of the competent ordinary.'
Domestic Prelate	An honour bestowed upon particular clerics by the Holy See. Recipients are usually styled 'Right Revd Monsignor' and may wear a more distinctive form of ceremonial attire than other clergy. Prior to the Second Council, domestic prelates had the right to use the *bugia* at Mass, a ceremonial candlestick with a short, straight handle.
Exorcism	From Greek, *to put on oath*. The ritual casting out of evil spirits. Lesser forms of exorcism are included in the ritual of Baptism.
Mass Cabin	Also referred to in sources as a Mass House or Chapel. These were wretchedly basic buildings used for worship by Catholics during the Penal era.
Mensal Parish	A parish where the bishop is the PP and has a CA or vicar who administers it on his behalf. The revenues from such parishes were, in former times, applied to the upkeep of the bishop.

Msgr	Monsignor. From the Italian *monseigneur* for *my lord*. An honorary title within the Church.
NS	National (though more properly Primary) School.
NT	National Teacher. A generic term for those who teach at Primary School level.
(Apostolic) Nuncio	The ambassador of the Holy See to a particular country or region.
ODC	Order of Discalced Carmelites.
Papal Bulls	A papal letter of solemn form and, in former times, sealed with a lead seal.
Penal Code	A series of laws enacted against Catholics, the first appearing in 1695, which banned Catholics from holding arms or being educated on the Continent. The last of these laws were repealed in 1829.
PP	Parish Priest.
Prior	A monastic superior who holds office for a set period.
Pro-cathedral	A church used by a diocese as the principal church until a worthier building can be erected. Throughout the nineteenth century, several newspaper reports refer to the building in Loughrea which is now Kilboy's Funeral Home as the Pro-cathedral of Clonfert diocese.
Professed	The admittance to vows, either simple or solemn, of members of a religious house or institution.
PTAA	Pioneer Total Abstinence Association.
Regular	Refers to clergy who are part of a community and live by a rule, as distinct from seculars, i.e. diocesan clergy.
Reliquary	A vessel in which items of a sacred nature are stored for protection and ease of transport.
Reredos	A sculpted or ornate screen of stone or wood to be found at the rear of a pre-Conciliar altar and which may be structurally part or discrete from the altar.
RIC	Royal Irish Constabulary.
Sexton	A sacristan or one who attends to the daily upkeep of a church and its goods.
SCA	Society of the Catholic Apostolate. Members are more commonly referred to as Pallotines after the founder, St Vincent Pallotti.
SMA	Society of African Missionaries.

Synod of Kells   Major Church synod held in 1152 at which Irish dioceses
                    were grouped into four provinces, i.e. Armagh, Dublin,
                    Cashel and Tuam.

Whit Sunday   An older term for Pentecost Sunday, the first Sunday
                    after Easter. The *Whit* was derived from the white
                    garments worn by those baptised during the Easter vigil.

1

MULLAGH AND KILLORAN

Formerly known as Abbeygormican and Killoran, it took its name from the abbey founded there for the Canons Regular of St Augustine under the invocation of the Virgin Mary. Dermod O'Feighen was prior there in 1309 and was sued by William Hackett for 5 acres of turbary in Corballynenegall. Richard de Valle also sued the prior for 54 acres of land with their appurtenances in Fynounta (Finnure). In 1534, Henry VIII granted the abbey to Ulick, 1st Earl of Clanricarde. Today its precincts are used as a cemetery and the remnant of the abbey until recently held one of the finest extant examples of a Jacobean tomb.

In the sacristy of St Brendan's church in Mullagh there is the top of a Penal-era altar inscribed with the name of the parish priest Fr John Dolan and the year 1760. An account book from Coen's of Eskerboy bears the name of Revd John Dolan who died in August 1828, so Dolan bids fair to have been the longest-serving parish priest on record in the diocese of Clonfert. He was obviously well established when Mullagh and Kilrickle were still united as one parish. This changed in 1809 when Killoran, which had been a parish in its own right, was annexed to Mullagh and Kilrickle was given to Cappatagle due to the not inconsiderable influence of the Donelan's of BallyDonelan. Cappatagle parish register records the main reason for the union, noting *'ob causam paupertatis'*, i.e. the cause was poverty. The people of Kilrickle, however, were not best pleased as they loved their old parish priest and when Fr McKeigue of Cappatagle came to celebrate his first Sunday Mass there, he found the doors and windows of Kilrickle chapel barred against him. A stalemate held for three weeks with the people demanding Dolan back but Bishop Thomas Costello would not budge. The matter was not aided by Dolan's residing just down the road from Kilrickle with his brother, in a house just opposite Finnure Cemetery. Eventually, the people relented. Though Mullagh church has been much modified since its erection in 1762, it is the only church in the diocese to be built in the Penal-era that is still in use. The parish has given several vocations to the diocese of Clonfert. Fr Pat Coen was from Eskerboy and was parish priest in Woodford during the heady days of the Land War. Fr Tom Coen, who died as parish priest of Aughrim in 1891, came from Abbeygormican. Others include Revd Briscoe from Castletown, Martin Larkin from Boleyroe, Ferdinand 'Fardy' Whyte from Corbally Beg, Peter Greaney from Bettaville, Killoran and Fintan Daly SMA from Poppyhill.

The parish is peppered with the remains of native enclosed settlements (more popularly called ringforts), once homesteads which were defended with wooden palisades. These were usually built on the principle of inter-visibility in the event of attack. Later, with the development of stone houses or wattle-and-daub cabins, these ringforts likely became regarded as the former dwellings of the ancestors which may be the origin of the belief that many were the haunts of fairy folk. A belief which runs deep in the rural Irish psyche is that to touch or interfere with a ringfort is to invite disaster upon one's head and to cut a lone bush is to incur the wrath of otherworldly beings. Some hold implicitly to belief in the *púca*, whom they claim roams Ballylogue in Killoran. This spirit was said to appear in the form of a horse and was given to running under people's legs to carry them away on a nightmarish gallop. Those venturing out at night wore steel spurs as a defence against the demon. The *púca* was also reputed to spit upon wild fruit in November in an act of otherworldly bad-mindedness, making it unsafe to eat. Locally, as in other parts of the diocese, there are tales of the *cóiste bodhar* or death coach, a carriage driven by a headless man whose wheels were so loud that even the deaf could hear them. The coach was taken as a portent of a death and those walking home late who heard it were advised to throw themselves prostrate and face down on the ground until it had passed. Folk beliefs generally had a germ of old wisdom embedded in them as Henry Morris noted in 1915. When a morsel of food fell to the ground, it was believed it should be left there for the fairies. The wisdom underpinning this belief was, of course, linked to hygiene given that old country floors were usually earthen and thus crawling with all manner of deadly microbe. The death coach and tales of things that went bump in the night were possibly linked to the necessity for belief in God and to prevent late-night ramblings by younger folk.

Fr Matthew Donohoe (1882–1934), who was a native of Heathlawn, Killimor and who erected the Sacred Heart window in Assumption Church, Killoran in 1913. He died in Kearney, Nebraska. (Courtesy of Clonfert Diocesan Archives)

Revd John and Pat O'Reilly, natives of Mullagh. (Courtesy of Mrs Joan Treacy)

Taken on the occasion of the confirmations at the Bishop's Chair, Ballylogue, 1976 with Bishop Thomas Ryan. Front row, from left to right: Kay Cahalan, Kathleen Hanrahan, Kathleen Hough, Caroline Glynn, Maura Kilkenny, Dolores Hobbins, Margaret Bugler, Aggie Finnerty, Marie Gallagher. Back row: Geraldine Daly, Geraldine Dolan, Bernie Finnerty, Evelyn Curley, Eithne Curley, Gabrielle Coen, Gabrielle Broderick, May Treacy. (Courtesy of Mrs Mary Kilkenny)

Taken on Whit Sunday, 1915. Fr Thomas O'Connor in military chaplain's uniform with his sister Ms Josephine O'Connor, NT. She joined the Sisters of Mercy in Middlesborough, England and became Sr Mary Finbar. She was not long for this world, however, and died on 14 June 1917 being professed on her deathbed. Some parishioners in Mullagh considered Fr O'Connor an austere and aloof figure but they forget the impact that his sister's death had on him, the awful sights he witnessed during the war and his own suffering with malaria. (Courtesy of Mr Eamon Hayes)

Sketch of Fr Thomas O'Connor as a Chaplain to the Forces. He was nicknamed 'TOC', after his initials. (Courtesy of Mr Eamon Hayes)

Killoran

Dedicated to St Oran, he was believed to be the charioteer of St Patrick and was martyred by being buried alive. In 1953 Revd Dr Kevin Egan interviewed 70-year-old Darby Byrnes who lived in Ballylogue. It was there that ordinations took place in the Penal-era which were presided over by Bishop Tadhg Keogh and latterly Bishop Murtagh Donelan. Behind Darby's home was a sycamore tree on the boundary of a paddock where a Penal church once stood with a priest's residence just to the north of it. He claimed that misfortune befell those who interfered with it. A few hundred yards south-west of this site is the spot known as *Cathaoir an Easpaig* where the ordinations took place. In 1976 Fr Peter Dunne had the place cordoned off with railings and a chair was made from grave-slabs by Johnnie Hardiman of Gortavoher townland. Bishop Thomas Ryan performed the confirmations there that year under an awning. When Bishop Dignan penned a history of the diocese in the early 1940s, he referred to the 'ordinations which had taken place in Penal days in the bogs of Killoran'. Having given a copy of the work to parish-native Fr Peter Greaney to proofread, his Lordship received it back with the offending line amended to read 'in a bog in Killoran'.

A modest dwelling ... the parochial house in Killoran, June 1943. Erected 1884—1886, the front rooms had high ceilings which aided ventilation in the days of smoky fires in large hearths and also gave a slightly grander appearance for guests. Two curates died while resident here, Fr Thomas Walsh in 1890 and Fr Peter Lee in 1903. The appendage just visible at the rear was the residence of the housekeeper until 1948 when the house was rebuilt. (Courtesy of Clonfert Diocesan Archives)

Bettaville House, Killoran. Built in Elizabethan times, this house served in the Penal-era as a refuge for Daniel Kelly, the Vicar-General of Clonfert diocese, and the few clergy brave enough to serve the parishes. Writing to Rome from here, Kelly pleaded '... our flame is almost extinguished'. Latterly, it was the house in which Fr Peter Greaney (1897–1953) was born. (Courtesy of Theo Hanley)

The bell of Killoran Church as it stood prior to 1954 when it was incorporated into the steeple of the newly built church. (Courtesy of Clonfert Diocesan Archives)

Folklore

There is a killuhuan or *lisín* in the townland of Drimatubber. It is believed that agents of Lord Trench drained the land in order to deprive the holy well there but the water sprang out of an ash tree instead. This well was attributed to St Brendan whom the people said rested there while on his travels. A pattern was also held at Oran's Well, known as *Tobar Oran*, though not within living memory. In reality it is simply the point at which three drains meet and is located to the rear of the parochial house in Killoran.

Killoran Mills gave the only steady employment up until the Second World War and slightly beyond. The only other work outside of farming was in the making of the roads. The mills were built by Healy's and owned successively by Scully's, Pelly's and finally Glynn's.

The first postal pillar box came to Killoran in 1894 and electrification did not arrive until 1955, people having to make do with tilly and hurricane lamps.

The church of 1837 was erected by Fr John Griffin and was used for a time as a school. It was at a station Mass in Malachy Kelly's in Ballylogue around 1840 that it was first proposed that it be slated, being at that time thatched, and so £1 per house was collected for that purpose, no mean feat in times

Parishioners at St Brendan's church, Mullagh greet Dr Dignan following confirmations, 8 June 1943. (Courtesy of Clonfert Diocesan Archives)

Parishioners at St Brendan's church, Mullagh greet Dr Dignan following confirmations,
8 June 1943; different detail. (Courtesy of Clonfert Diocesan Archives)

prior to the Famine. The chapel had been constructed and partly slated by
a man called Curley from Ballylogue. When the church was being rebuilt
in 1953, six brick-lined graves were unearthed in the sanctuary. As the
post-Reformation church also stood on the same site, it is likely these were
the graves of clergy who served the parish up until the 1830s.

The curate's residence, which is among the smallest in the diocese of Clonfert,
was commenced in 1884 and completed in 1886, the first resident being Fr James
Cahalan. It was started by William Glynn of Springfield, who died shortly into
the project, and completed by two masons called Flanagan and Lysaght. Thomas
Pelly also claimed that around 1861 he went to Ballinasloe with his parents and
bought the first wall oil lamp known in 'the valley'.

Schooling

Three hedge schools are recalled in this district, with one in a small house
belonging to John O'Gorman in Clare Road and run by Frances Martyn and
her father. After the father's death, Frances continued by herself. She was a
native of Duniry and lodged at neighbouring houses. About forty children
attended the school. At weekends Miss Martyn would go home and the people

Dr Dignan, Fr Thos O'Connor PP and contractor standing in the shell of the new Mullagh school, June 1943. (Courtesy of Clonfert Diocesan Archives)

Mullagh parochial house, erected in 1886 by Fr Joseph Bodkin PP. It was in the front room that Bishop John Healy was standing when three men from Killoran tried to kill him by firing a shot through the window. (Courtesy of Clonfert Diocesan Archives)

would give her tea, sugar and bread to take with her. Beyond these kindnesses, she received no other remuneration. She moved the school from Clare to Cormack townland into a small house on John Briscoe's farm but *d'fhág sí an ceantar* around 1880, returning to Duniry where she died. A third school operated at Springfield, Killoran, under the auspices of Mr Sullivan. According to Thomas Pelly of Springfield, Killoran (aged 78 in 1931), he went to school in a mud cabin in Springfield run by Mr Sullivan and Mr Bermingham, both natives of Lusmagh, Banagher. This was around 1860 and there were some forty pupils. The charge was one penny per week. Sullivan had a married son named Barney and two daughters, Maggie and Nancy and the latter married a soldier. Afterwards, a Tyrol McMahon taught school in the chapel at Killoran but went begging and died in the workhouse. Sullivan lodged for a time with the Pelly's. An obsolete form of punishment from Thomas Pelly's childhood was to put one child on another's back for caning. Pelly claimed that the first resident of Springfield was a man called Spring, hence came the name of the townland.

Under the Road

When the hill on the road outside the old teacher's residence in Mullagh was being cut, two skeletons were found. They were reinterred on the side of the road at a stile leading into the well opposite the residence which itself has remained unoccupied for some time.

Castellated Houses

Castlenancy Castle was spread across two adjoining fields in Castlenancy townland. The owner was Nancy Daly, but this was prior to there being a village there and at that time, we are informed, the townland was called Béal átha na n-éan or the mouth of the ford of the birds. The last owner of the castle died in 1815 and it became ruinous, its remnants now peppering the field-walls and older tenant dwellings of the townland. At that time there were only about sixteen or seventeen houses in the townland though at the time of the Ordnance Survey in 1838, O'Donovan stated that there were only 'a few'.

Older people believed that there was a river or canal flowing from Castlenancy to Abbeygormican and that some of the stones of the castle were brought to build the church that is now in ruins there.

Julia and Malachy Kelly, Ballylogue, *c*. 1935. It was Malachy Kelly's grandfather who suggested the slating of Killoran Church at a station in the townland in 1833. The mowing machine was considered quite a bit of technology in its day. Drawn by a horse and fitted with blades, it was a far more leisurely manner of mowing. These machines first appeared in Ireland around 1900. (Courtesy of Mr Dermot and Mrs Angela Donohue)

The Bishop's Chair, Ballylogue, constructed in 1976 by Johnnie Hardiman, Gortavoher. It is made of headstones while the altar top is of a ledger. The spot was reputed to be where the Penal-era ordinations were performed but this was conjectural. (Courtesy of Theo Hanley)

Ballyfintan Castle stood on Fahey's land and was believed to originate with Fintan, an eighth-century Norseman. Shortly after his death, his wife was murdered there under a hawthorn bush by Irish chieftains.

An obscure tradition notes a castle at Corbally which in the late nineteenth century was dismantled and used in boundary walls.

Industry

While the main employer up to and slightly beyond the years of the Emergency was Killoran Mills, linen manufacture was still a vital cog in the local economy of the nineteenth century, with several families growing their own flax. It was then prepared and spun for the weaver. The Whelan's and Hanrahan's of Castlenancy were known as extensive flax growers. By 1930, linen wheels were still to be found in Cormican's of Cappanaughton, Coen's of Lurgan and Kilkenny's of Lurgan. Warping bars and hackler were to be found at that time in Hobbins's of Gurtymadden. Mullagh had three weavers, namely Reid of Gurtymadden, Mrs Hanrahan of Boleyroe and Mulkerrin of Hollyhill. Reid was the principal weaver and had the help of two sons.

More economically beneficial than linen was the carding, spinning and weaving of wool and each person wore their own tweed and frieze (a shaggy, woollen fabric). Woollen spinning wheels dotted the parish until about seventy years back and the wool was coloured with *barróg*s (branches of a certain tree which grew in Woodford) and bog-black. The *barróg*s were boiled for two days and two nights in a huge pot called the colouring pot. Only one such receptacle existed in Gurtmadden and was owned by a man called Gavin.

Poitín Galore! Cigarettes not so Galore

An illegal still existed until around 1870 at John Fitzgerald's in Foxhall and another at Kitty Duggan's in Ballyfintan. The law at the time was obviously more honoured in the breach than in the observance, as the local constabulary actually assisted in its distilling. It was sold for 1s 6d per pint and Kitty often walked with a supply to Galway and back on the same day. The more stately beverage of tea first came to Mullagh around 1860, a good 250 years after the Dutch first introduced it to Europe. A novel but ill-judged enterprise was

St Brendan's church, Mullagh. Erected in 1762, it is the only church built in the Penal-era in the diocese to be still used for worship. (Courtesy of Clonfert Diocesan Archives)

Dr Dignan administering confirmation, 8 June 1943 in Mullagh. From left to to right: Revd John O'Connor, Pat Cuffe, Larry Moran, John Kenny O'Neill. (Courtesy of Clonfert Diocesan Archives)

the growing of tobacco leaves by one Pat Hanrahan who lived at Castlenancy. A 'returned yank', he brought with him large amounts of tobacco leaf and attempted to plant it from seed but the leaves never attained great size and the project was abandoned.

Card Sharks and the Musical Genius of Denny Delaney

Card playing is still a popular pastime and until the years of the Second World War, one could expect to find fowl, bonhams, sheep, onions and even socks as gambling material. Some *pisreoga* surrounded the game such as how the placing of a needle in a person's coat without their knowledge was believed to bring good luck. Changing places with partners also brought a change in luck while lending or counting your winnings prior to a game boded ill. Card games included Twenty-Five, Fifteen, Solo and Nap.

Other forms of entertainment included music. Denny Delaney, a piper who hailed from Tulrush in Ballinasloe, was remembered clearly by locals until recent years as he played at virtually every dance. This musical genius deserves a few lines in remembrance. Struck blind by smallpox at the age of 13, he had acquired a gift for the Irish pipes at this stage and at

Dr Dignan and assisting clergy in St Brendan's church, Mullagh, 8 June 1943. The High Altar and reredos was originally in St Michael's church, Ballinasloe but was donated to Mullagh in the 1920s. (Courtesy of Clonfert Diocesan Archives)

The redoubtable Dr John Healy, Bishop of Clonfert 1896–1903. He had a close shave while staying at Mullagh parochial house. (Courtesy of Clonfert Diocesan Archives)

Fr Pascal Donohoe (1937–2005) a native of Cormack townland. Pascal was ordained in 1964 at the Basilica of St John Lateran, at that time the first priest of Clonfert diocese to be ordained in Rome for twenty-five years. (Courtesy of Fr Pascal's family)

56 years of age in 1897, he defeated Martin O'Reilly, the champion piper of Connacht, at a pipers' competition in Galway. He would go on to play at the Queen's Theatre and at the Covent Garden Theatre in London and by the end of his remarkable life, his total prizes numbered forty-four firsts, sixteen seconds and six thirds. In 1916 he was arrested in Mountbellew for playing 'seditious' tunes, but released within a short time. What a curious thought, that the musical prowess of this humble little man sans sight should threaten the might of the British Empire! A small plaque commemorates him at the entrance to what was once 'Bolger's Lane' at the top of Main Street in Ballinasloe.

Lost Similes

Some lesser-known similes from former years include:

As crooked as a ram's horn
As dark as a dungeon or a bag

As yellow as a duck's foot
As clever as a judge
As ignorant as a bag of brogues
As drunk as a stick
As tough as a gad (a pointed tool used in breaking rocks)
As supple as an eel
As grey as a badger
As old as a bush
As cross as a bag of cats
As old as Methuselah's cat (the owner being claimed by the Book of Genesis to have lived to the age of 969)
And the still current as hard as flint and as bold as brass

Pisreoga on Death

Then, as now, death was a grave affair (no pun intended) and required the strict observance of old beliefs. The crowing of a cock at unusual hours was always a portent of death. If rigor mortis didn't set in quickly, another member of the family might well die soon. An odd number of candles were lit in the corpse room, mirrors were covered (for fear of catching a glimpse of the spirit of the deceased) and house clocks were stopped. To meet a funeral brought bad luck unless you took a few steps with the cortege in the direction of the cemetery. The bier that brought the coffin to the place of burial was to be destroyed. A grave could never be opened on Mondays. Finally, no short cut could be taken to the cemetery in the belief that the longest route would confuse a spirit bent on returning to haunt or wreak vengeance on the living. Few if any of these customs have survived into the twenty-first century, though the last mentioned is still observed in Killoran out of respect for custom.

Weather Portents

A dog eating grass was a portent of rain and if the cat sat with his back to the fire, then it was time to get the umbrella out!

2

LOUGHREA

The town of Loughrea takes its name from the lake which is often referred to as the grey lake or Loch Riabhach. The changing colours of its shores (caused by the reflection of the lake's white sandy or marshy bottom) gives grounds for this interpretation. However, in an old document called the *Dinnsheanchas* or the *Lore of Places,* another interpretation is given. The passage runs thus:

> Lough Riach; from whence did it get its name? The answer is not difficult. Four kings held sway in Maenmach whose names were Caimeall and Edar and Casta and Riach. Caimeall indeed had a daughter and Edar another. Casta and Riach wooed these princesses but their suit was neglected. They then declared war on Caimeall and Eder but none survived the battle but Riach alone, from whom is named Loch Riach, in which he was afterwards drowned.

Legend has it that Loch Riach was one of those lakes which suddenly appeared in old Ireland. Roderick O'Flaherty, the Galway man, relates that in 2937 BC it began to overflow and the *Four Masters* record that in the year of the world 3506 'Loch Riach burst forth'. Due to the belief that so much blood had been spilled on its shores, the waters of the lake had the reputation of dyeing sheep's wool red. As the *Dinnsheanchas* relates, 'It was customary to drive sheep of all Ireland every seventh year into it ...' Five miles in circumference, the lake is said to be supplied by seven distinct springs, once called the Seven Sisters, and this is the source of yet another origin legend. A poor man longed to own a horse but lacking the financial resources, he set his heart on one fine mare that belonged to the fairies. While the good folk were feasting, he stole their horse and as he had bested them they told him he could keep it for a year and a day but only on condition that it never saw the sun set on Galway Bay. Overjoyed, the man entered the horse in the Knockbarron Races and won successive contests. Hitting for home, he unwisely chose to rest on Monument Hill and in the distance the sun

began to set. The brilliant glow from Galway Bay blinded his mount and it bounded down the hill in seven huge leaps. From each spot its hooves hit, there gushed a spring and each flowed down the hill to form the great lake. Lurking beneath the surface of the lake and adding to its mystique are the remains of five crannóg's, defended lake-dwellings established on artificial islands in medieval times.

The old parish church or Pro-cathedral of Loughrea which is now Kilboy's Funeral Home. The date it was built is unknown but an inscription on the font, which is preserved in the funeral parlour, reads 'Repaired by Revd Dr Myler Burke 1786', providing a *terminus ante quem* for the building. A stone in the grounds displayed a mitre and the date '1843' which likely refers to Dr Coen's renovation of the church. Tower and belfry were erected 1843–4. The church had two galleries with the 'Grand Gallery' on the right occupied by the better-off of the parish. A caretaker called Biddy ensured that only the correct pew-holders took their seat there. The main door was, according to an account by a long-dead parishioner, for the 'collarless, the sinners, the saints, the frieze coats and the shawls'. It was deconsecrated shortly after 1905. (Courtesy of Clonfert Diocesan Archives)

The last extant remnant of the medieval town of Loughrea, dating from the fifteenth century. Privately occupied until the late 1940s, it was later home to the Diocesan Museum. The graffiti appears to be cheap advertising for a political candidate rather than vandalism. (Courtesy of Clonfert Diocesan Archives)

Loughrea was a walled and ditched garrison town. The enclosed town was rectangular, having four entrance gates, two of which stood at the northern and southern extremities of the town and were named respectively Mob Hill and Latimer Gates. The lake, running along the whole of the south side, made access by an invading force impossible. Strong castles stood sentry over each entrance and one is extant. These fortifications were established in 1232 by Richard de Burgo who had received grants of land in Connacht. The de Burgos were to become the Earls of Clanricarde, their other chief residences outside of Loughrea being Kilcooley and Portumna.

The Carmelites

The old Carmelite Abbey dates back to 1300 when it was established by Richard de Burgo III (died 1326) who was also known as the Red Earl of Ulster. The ruins of the old Abbey are in an excellent state of preservation and a tradition holds that General Charles Chalmont, also known as the Marquis Saint-Ruth, was buried beneath the tower following his decapitation at the Battle of Aughrim. The retreating Jacobites entered Loughrea at midnight via Boithrín Com and found the inhabitants fleeing into the Sliabh Aughty mountains for refuge. Six friars were witnesses to the hasty obsequies for Chalmont which were performed by torchlight. The friary was suppressed during the reign of Henry VIII and granted to the Earl of Clanricarde. The foundation of Carmelite nuns at Loughrea dates from 1680. A young lady of noble birth, Eleanor Bourke, expressed an ardent desire to become a Carmelite nun and as she was a descendant of the Red Earl, a house was provided near St Brigid's Well, now believed to be St Bride's on Bride Street. The Vicar Provincial of the Carmelite Order, Fr James Brichlane, approved of Eleanor's piety and she became the first nun to take the habit in Loughrea, receiving the name in religion of Sr Mary Teresa of St Dominic. Over the next fifty or so years, three new houses were established in Limerick, Dublin and Cork. Mother Teresa awaits the Resurrection inside the walls of the old Carmelite Abbey and near the vault of the Dolphin family.

In 1765, after sixty-five years at Bride Street, the location of the convent moved to Main Street which at that time was called High Street. In the early 1800s they moved yet again to the location now occupied by the Sisters of Mercy in Cross Street and in 1830 a site was purchased from the Marquess of Clanricarde. Comprising of 10 acres, it is now known as St Joseph's, Mount

The oldest extant image of clergy of the diocese, taken in early 1864 at what appears to be the Carmelite Abbey. Many of the individuals depicted were pillars of the diocese in their own time. From left to right: Revd John Sellars (died 1877 as parish priest of Carrabane), Joseph Bodkin (died 1897 as parish priest of Mullagh), Msgr James Madden (died 1901 as parish priest of Tynagh), Thomas Coen (died 1891 as parish priest of Aughrim), Laurence Murphy ODC, Thomas Pelly (died 1883 as parish priest of Kiltullagh), James Hynes (died 1883 as parish priest of Duniry), Andrew Griffin (died 1884 as parish priest of Leitrim), Fr Russell ODC, Msgr Thomas Burke (died 1884 as parish priest of Portumna), John Callaghy (died 1890 as parish priest of Ballinakill), Dr Derry, Michael Mahon ODC, John Macklin (died 1871 as parish priest of Carrabane), Michael Mullins (died in Chicago in 1869). (Courtesy of Clonfert Diocesan Archives)

Carmel. Though involved in education for a short period after Catholic Emancipation, since the mid-nineteenth century the nuns have observed their contemplative rule. One notable feature of the chapel at Mount Carmel is that it acts as the resting place of the remains of St Amantius, a second-century martyr of Rome. His remains, along with a phial of his blood, were the gift of Pope Gregory XVI in 1841 to Dr Thomas Coen, Bishop of Clonfert. In 1981, the casket containing the martyr's bones were placed within the new altar in the chapel.

Some Carmelite natives of the diocese died in ministry abroad, including Fr Boniface Nevin of Woodford who died in Africa in 1899, Fr Elias Pelly of Killimor who died in India in 1871 and Fr Peter Burke of Derrybrien who died in Baghdad in 1905.

The Abbey ruin as seen on a postcard, *c.* 1926. General Saint-Ruth, who commanded the Jacobite army at Aughrim, reputedly rests beneath the tower. After the defeat, the Jacobite forces were said to have entered Loughrea via Bohercom about midnight and found the inhabitants had fled into the Aughties for refuge. (Courtesy of Clonfert Diocesan Archives)

Reflecting on the world to come … Fr Damian Nolan (1912–2005) ODC in contemplation among the graves of the Carmelite Abbey Cemetery. (Courtesy of J.J. Broderick)

The Sisters of Mercy

With a legacy of £1,000 from Mrs Whyte of Loughrea, Dr Derry invited the Sisters of Mercy from Baggot Street in Dublin to begin a foundation in his diocese. There being no sisters available from Dublin, he sent a petition to Tullamore and five sisters were promised. These sisters took up residence in Hardiman's of Barrack Street in September of 1850 and Mother Catherine McCauley was to spend a night there en route to Galway. This house stood on the corner of Moore and Cross Street and is now part of the playground of St Ita's Primary School. Initially, the Sisters served the ill and dying in small hospitals on Cross Street and Barrack Street and a school was established in a building called the Brewery. In March 1853, Sr Magdalen Burke created a foundation at Ballinasloe and the Sisters resided in a house on Main Street. Dr Derry laid the foundation stone of the Convent Chapel in Loughrea in August of 1857 and the first Mass was celebrated there in March 1858. An orphanage, latterly called an industrial school, was opened in 1864 and closed in 1967. Dr Duggan would lay the foundation stone of the present Convent of Mercy in Loughrea on 9 September 1877 and it was completed in 1879. There were further establishments in Portumna in 1882, Woodford in 1900 and Eyrecourt in 1901.

Fr Patrick Winters and Dr Dignan being greeted by the Revd Mother at St Raphael's, 1945. (Courtesy of Clonfert Diocesan Archives)

St Raphael's Convent. (Courtesy of Clonfert Diocesan Archives)

Sr Gertrude Smyth
(1896–1984) in the old
habit of the Sisters of
Mercy. She was the last
member of the Smyth
family of Masonbrook who
owned some 30,000 acres
in the county of Galway in
the nineteenth century. Her
family was linked to many
notable figures including
Edward Martyn, Lord
Dunsandle and Sir Thomas
Burke of Marblehill.
(Courtesy of Clonfert
Diocesan Archives)

The Carmelite Sisters gather with Rt Revd Msgr Cathal Geraghty and parishioners on the occasion of the visit of St Terese's relics to Loughrea, 10 June 2001. (Courtesy of Clonfert Diocesan Archives)

A doll's house fit for a queen. In what was known as 'the baby room' in the Convent of Mercy. (Courtesy of Clonfert Diocesan Archives)

The Parish

Little is known of the old parish, but the cemetery of Garrybreeda provides a few clues. The ruins of St Brigid's church there dates to around 1240 and once preserved there was St Brigid's Shoe, a brass reliquary bearing the

Corpus Christi procession led by Dr Dignan, *c.* 1925. (Courtesy of Clonfert Diocesan Archives)

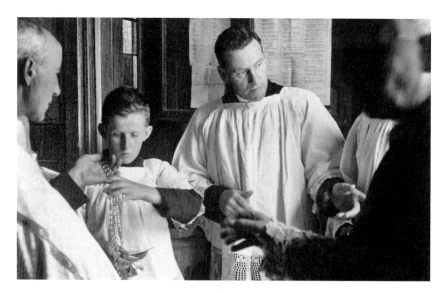

Fr Patrick Jennings, CA Loughrea 1924–1947, seen here as MC at a confirmation in Leitrim parish in May 1944. From left to right: Revd Dr John O'Connor PP, Kevin Hardiman (Newtowndaly), Fr Jennings and Dr Dignan. (Courtesy of Clonfert Diocesan Archives)

inscription 'Loch Reich Anno Domini 1410. S. Brigida Virgo Kildariensis Hiberniae Patrona'. This sacred relic is now in the care of the National Museum. The church was of a modest size (22½ feet wide and 50½ feet long) and had an aumbry, still extant, in the right-hand corner of the east gable.

The building now housing Kilboy's Funeral Home was once the Pro-cathedral. Whilst it had been re-slated and a tower and belfry were erected by Bishop Coen in 1843, within a couple of decades it had become inadequate to the needs of the local population. Patrick Duggan, who became bishop in 1871, was never tired of bewailing the fact that he could not build a new cathedral, though he had a formidable foe. The Marquess of Clanricarde continually obstructed Duggan in his quest to find a suitable site, even though Duggan had £3,000 in hand as the nucleus of a fund. Eventually a site was found but Dr Duggan was to die a year before the foundation stone was laid. His successor, Bishop John Healy, was to hold Clanricarde in similar disdain, claiming he had 'done more to bring the ancient name of Clanricarde into shame and dishonour than all those who have gone before him put together'.

Fr Hyacinth O'Callaghan CA 1949–1973. Born in Kiltormer, Laurencetown to John and Mary (née Davy) O'Callaghan on 8 August 1913, he was educated at Garbally Park. In his senior years, he played the principal baritone roles of Archibald Grosvenor in *Patience* and Lord Mountararat in *Iolanthe*, the lesser performed Gilbert and Sullivan operettas. In the latter production were some future priests of the diocese in the guise of earls, including Hugh Flynn and Larry Moran. Ordained in 1939, he spent a short curacy in Hexham and Newcastle diocese and then became CC Loughrea 1943–1949. He became CA after Fr Thomas Murphy moved to Ballinakill. Known as 'Fr O', he was involved in all aspects of life in Loughrea, from the Anglers' Association to rugby and GAA. He was diocesan secretary from 1949, one of his last functions being to accompany Bishop Thomas Ryan to Rome. He died suddenly on 19 July 1973 and was the first burial in cathedral grounds since that of Fr Michael Griffin in 1922. At the time of his death he was working on a history of the cathedral. Poignantly, there was an echo of his earlier years in Garbally; he had been listening to the audiotape of the musical *Camelot* in his car, as it was the forthcoming production of the Loughrea Musical Society. (Courtesy of Marie Lyons)

The old presbytery on Barrack Street. Built in 1903, it was demolished in 1997. (Courtesy of Clonfert Diocesan Archives)

St Brendan's Cathedral

The foundation stone for the new cathedral was laid and blessed by Dr Healy on 10 October 1897. Though he had initially thought to have St Michael's church in Ballinasloe as his cathedral church, he was persuaded by Edward Martyn among others, to plump for Loughrea. Martyn, who was a native of Loughrea, had founded the Feis Cheoil in 1896 and in 1902 founded the Palestrina Choir. St Brendan's was to become a treasure trove of the Celtic Revival. Another major factor in the success of the project was the energy and enthusiasm of Fr Jeremiah O'Donovan, a curate in the parish and latterly the administrator. The first public function to be held in the cathedral was the solemn consecration of Bishop Thomas O'Dea on 30 August 1903. A week later, three young men were ordained priest within its sanctuary, one of them a future bishop of the diocese, Dr John Dignan.

Confirmation Day at the Cathedral, 1945. (Courtesy of Clonfert Diocesan Archives)

Dr Dignan arriving for confirmation ceremony, 1945. (Courtesy of Clonfert Diocesan Archives)

Cast and inscription on the Fr Michael Griffin Memorial Monument in the grounds of St Brendan's Cathedral. A native of Gurteen, Fr Griffin was murdered in November 1920, while on loan to Galway diocese. Many considered it the work of the Black and Tans, but his biographer, the late Archdeacon Paddy Lee, discovered that the fatal shot was fired by a member of the RIC. (Courtesy of Theo Hanley)

The Fr Michael Griffin Memorial Monument, St Brendan's Cathedral, marking where
Fr Griffin is buried. (Courtesy of Theo Hanley)

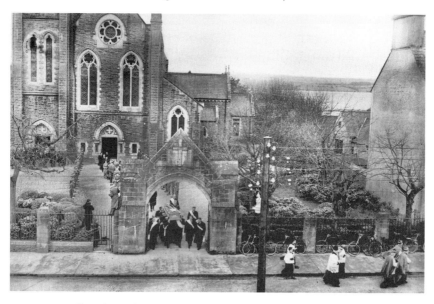

Dr Dignan's coffin is borne from the cathedral to Mount Pleasant Cemetery. (Courtesy of Sean Cleary)

Dr Dignan's funeral turning the corner of Church Street, past Leahy's Shop to the right of view. The men flanking the coffin usually carried the canopium for the Corpus Christi procession and are Seámus Kennedy (front left), Charlie Kelly, an eggler on Barrack Street (back left) and Frank O'Brien, Mt Pleasant (back right). (Courtesy of Sean Cleary)

Fr Thomas Nohilly, CA of St Brendan's Cathedral 1898–1901. A native of Cummer, County Galway, he matriculated into 1st Philosophy, Maynooth for the archdiocese of Tuam on 4 September 1884 and was ordained in Portumna on 25 March 1890 by Bishop John Healy as he was to serve on loan to Clonfert. How he was chosen is unknown but his being a native of the same parish as Bishop Duggan may have played a role. He liked the diocese well enough to stay and after curacies in Ballinakill, Woodford, Ballinasloe and Loughrea, he succeeded to Lusmagh as parish priest in 1901, remaining there until his death. He built the current parochial house there and promoted the Irish language, even leading classes in the early years of his pastorate. In July 1910, he was one of a number of clergymen seriously injured when a morning train from Birr collided with an excursion train 5 miles outside Roscrea, throwing Nohilly to the floor of the carriage in which he was seated. Despite his injuries, a short holiday seemed to cure most ills. Something of a trencherman, he weighed in at 25 stone and was considered by his fellow clergy to be socially worth every ounce of his avoirdupois. Two brothers were members of Tuam District Council while another worked at the Waldorf-Astoria Hotel in New York. A grand-nephew was Fr Sean Higgins, late parish priest of Kilkerrin. He died 22 June 1926. (Courtesy of Fr Phil Hearty)

Patrick Duggan, Bishop of Clonfert 1871–1896. For the duration of his episcopate, he resided in Loughrea and it was during his ministry as a parish priest during the Famine that he became acutely conscious of the suffering of his people. He established a diocesan college in Loughrea and a classical school in Ballinasloe. The former produced twenty priests for Clonfert diocese and seven Carmelites. In his time too, he saw the railway line arrive at Loughrea and when the Famine of 1879 struck, it was through his foresight in securing turnip seed that many of his flock survived. He was called 'the poor man's bishop' and spent what spare time he had in the confessional or at parish devotions. Advancing years, however, weighed heavily on the latter part of his episcopate and he had never recovered fully from the stress induced by the trial before Judge William Keogh. One of the final straws was when, during a visit to Loughrea by Wilfred and Lady Anne Blunt, police attacked the crowd who had gathered to cheer them. Some women who sought refuge in the front hall of Dr Duggan's palace in Bride Street, were pursued and batoned by a number of constables as the old prelate watched helplessly. Dr Duggan is interred in Glasnevin Cemetery beside his old friend and classmate, Cardinal Edward McCabe. (Courtesy of Clonfert Diocesan Archives)

John Derry, Bishop of Clonfert
1847–1870. When he moved from
Cartron, Cappatagle in 1863,
he resided in a house owned by
Major-General Benjamin Crispin,
a prominent English Catholic.
The location of this house is unknown.
(Courtesy of Clonfert Diocesan
Archives)

Ghost Stories

A number of tales of the supernatural have been preserved as part of the
local lore. One concerns the little church of St Brigid in Garrybreeda. A man
named Coy from the Galway Road used to drive to work up 'the Hill' along
the Ballinasloe road. On returning at night and while passing St Brigid's
church, invariably his sidecar lights would be blown out. This happened on
many occasions until one night he decided to bring a local priest. When they
reached the church, a hole in the road opened and flames began to shoot out.
The priest began to recite prayers with the result that the flames vanished
back into the earth and the hole sealed itself shut. Coy's lamps were never
blown out again.

Not even the Sisters of Mercy were safe from the paranormal and from
the site of the old school building on Cross Street was often heard the sound
of gunshots. In a room in the convent, which was once the chapel, a very

holy young girl was once passing when she felt her leg bound by chains. On invoking the name of the Blessed Virgin Mary, she felt herself released and the next day woke up to find a nice new blue ribbon beside her.

Another tale concerns John Dennis who was master of the famed pack of hounds called the Galway Blazers. Originally called the Galway Hunt, it acquired its distinctive name when the mansion which had given the hunt members shelter on one occasion caught fire and was consumed in the ensuing blaze. Dennis was of a kindly disposition, yet after his death a story began to circulate that his ghost was to be seen on moonlit nights galloping around the fields of Raford and Carnamuck, replete with three unearthly hounds.

Cloran's of Loughrea

Dr Cloran resided at what was to become known as the Railway Hotel and which was more recently O'Dea's Hotel. His brother John Joe had an apothecaries shop but owing to doubts about his qualifications he had to take on a full-time assistant. When he died, his effects were auctioned by Michael Nevin and his stock of bottles, which were bought by Dr Burke of Main Street, were until the 1930s to be seen in the Medical Hall of Dr Crowly, who married Dr Burke's widow. Cloran's assistant's name is, alas, not known but he was regarded as a great self-advertiser and had a large practice in a house in Moore Street which was latterly occupied by Mrs Monaghan. When going to attend a fracture case he would have the top of his carriage covered with splints in order to impress the townspeople and once accurately predicted that a woman he saw washing on the street would be dead the following day. Sure enough she was, from a haemorrhage it is said, and this greatly enhanced his reputation. Dr Cloran himself had a colourful, if not strained career. On 17 January 1861, he was called upon by the guardians of the workhouse to resign as medical officer (for an unknown reason) and in 1868 was prosecuted for £500 in damages by one Mrs Cogan, residing at Granby Row, Dublin. Cloran had set her up in a boarding house in Dublin on condition that she kept a room for him to stay in on his visits. In January of 1867, he visited and demanded the right to employ a servant girl there, which Mrs Cogan resented.

Education

There was a school for young ladies at Church Lane known as Miss Gibbons's in a house owned by the Ridge family. Miss Gibbons also did private teaching as a visiting governess and subsequently lived at McGee's on the Hill. Another private teacher was Professor Cummins who lived at Quirke's, Galway Road, but he was turned out for non-payment of rent. Urchins in the street used to annoy him by calling out 'Hic, hac, hoc!' Another house-to-house teacher was Tom King. Brawley's School had a distinguished scholar in Michael Concannon, B.L., M.A. He was later assistant at the school. Two former pupils of hedge schools were alive in Loughrea until the 1920s. One was John McHugh of Kelly's Lane who attended a school held in a barn and accessed via a ladder. Another was Polly Quirke of Abbey Lane who was a dressmaker and because of her gaunt countenance was called 'Copper-faced Quirke'. Hedge schools were generally comprised of a relatively dry spot in a ditch, cleared and slightly excavated until it resembled the foundation of a house. Sometimes sods were laid like blocks but the structure, if it can be called such, was generally of an ephemeral nature.

Exterior view of St Brendan's National School, 1945. (Courtesy of Clonfert Diocesan Archives)

St Brendan's Boys School, corridor, 1945. (Courtesy of Clonfert Diocesan Archives)

Dr Dignan quizzes the boys on their catechesis at St Brendan's National School. Rear: Fr Jennings CA, Msgr Patrick Winters SCA and Br Declan Murphy. Br Declan, who was a native of County Cork, qualified as a teacher in 1925 and died in 1983. (Courtesy of Clonfert Diocesan Archives)

Distant view of the St Brendan's Boys National School on Pigott's Street. Built in 1905, it was demolished in 1993 and the site was used to erect a district office for the ESB. (Courtesy of Pat Barrett)

No safety helmets here! Workers take a break during the building of what is now St Ita's Primary School, 1930. In the background is Bishop John Derry's Celtic Memorial. (Courtesy of Pat Barrett)

In matters of religion there was strict segregation in education as with worship and creed and there were two ladies schools for adherents of the Church of Ireland. One was run by two sisters, the Misses Blood and the other by a Miss Curran. The latter was much sought after as it was claimed she had a cure for the pernicious malady called Scrofula which was a form of tuberculosis affecting the lymph nodes of the neck. It was popularly called the King's Evil as from medieval times it was believed it could be cured by the touch of a monarch. The curriculum included old favourites such as needlework, pianoforte and French. Musical pieces for after-dinner enjoyment included such well-forgotten compositions as *Lord Combermere's March* and *The Battle of Prague*.

A Classical School was run by Mr Michael Winter and had Latin and Greek as its mainstays, but Winter's enterprise became a victim of the Famine, with many students dying and he was obliged to depart from the district to seek another living.

Former Residents

As with all things, names once well known get forgotten as time passes and families die off. Loughrea had many such families. The Ridge family resided at the Hill, in a house which was latterly Leonard's. James Ridge Snr had three children. James was a clerical student who entered Maynooth for Clonfert diocese in 1857 but left without taking Orders and travelled the world. In less enlightened times, it was a mark of opprobrium for a clerical student to leave the seminary and those who did so became known in many circles as 'spoiled priests' (much like a cloth that one spills liquid on or tarnishes in some way). Such was the prejudice against them that they were usually obliged never to return home again. *Castigat ridendo mores!* James Ridge had good enough memories of Clonfert to write a short verse for the *Loughrea Journal* in 1880 in which he reminisced about his time at the minor seminary:

Neath thy roof, dear Rus-in-Urbe,
Peace and plenty on me smiled.
And mingled pain and pleasure,
Fond remembrance oft recalls.
The happy years I spent in boyhood,
In St Brendan's College halls.

Pleasure at the thought of studies,
My kind masters made so sweet.
Pain to think that my old schoolmates,
In this world I ne'er shall meet.
Walsh, McDermott, Moran, Airly,
Should you see this verse of mine,
Let your hearts to mine responsive,
Thrill with thoughts of auld Lang Syne.

Thomas Ridge died of his wounds near the river Nive, Bayonne, during the Peninsular War (1808–1814) while serving with the Royal York Rangers. He had served as a captain with the 18th Portugese Line. Miss Mary Ridge lived at what was later Salmon's house, Bride Street. Four members of the Ridge family are buried at the Carmelite Abbey. These are Belinda (1758–1832), Captain James Thomas (1787–1813), Joseph (1800–1854) and Michael (1767–1845).

Jack Mullarville lived at Breeklough with his parents and grandfather. After his father died, the house in which he lived collapsed due to dilapidation and he was obliged to move with his mother into the workhouse. He always carried a whip and was said to have used it as liberally as his tongue. After his death the whip was placed in his coffin and the funeral was quite large. Mullarville was wont to eat raw meat and on one occasion ate a fisherman's catch of broach at Breeklough. A portly man, he often addressed people as 'My buff', his version of 'My good fellow'. It is possible he derived this from the name 'the Buffs' given to the Royal East Kent Regiment from the colour of their coat-facings and waistcoats, though the buff colour deriving from leather tanning is a more likely source, given that there was a tannery in Loughrea.

Yet another well-known soul was Mathias or Matty Coyne who lived at the convent gate lodge and was a fisherman. He was regarded as an authority for the shooting fraternity on how to approach a duck when shooting. He is listed in the 1841 Census, aged 50 and was grandfather of the late Sonny Barrett. Larry Smith of Earlspark was known to have been descended from a man who fought at the Battle of Aughrim. Michael Tanney drove the mail car from Woodlawn to Loughrea twice a day. He was a driver at Nevin's Hotel and died in Woodlawn in 1918, aged 104. In *Shraughaun a Crisha* (near the old rectory in Cross Street) there lived Major Charles Lynes who was regarded as an overbearing eccentric. Possessed of a striking resemblance to the Duke of Wellington, he dressed in a not dissimilar manner and would not permit women to even enter his dwelling. He would even rebuke his dog, while on walks, for consorting with common dogs. He kept a fox and an eagle as pets. A native of Middlesex, he died in 1858 and is interred in the grounds of Loughrea Church. His stately house was dynamited in 1965 to make way for the estate now known as Mount Pleasant.

Coorheen house, built for the Dowager Clancarty and finished in May 1862 for the princely sum of £3,275. The architect was James Forth Kempster (1816–1893), who also designed the lodges for Garbally House, the Railway Hotel in Ballinasloe and many of the later buildings at what was known as the Ballinasloe Lunatic Asylum. In building Coorheen House, the masons used the stones of the former defended dwelling of 'Blind Davy Power'. David Power had been High Sheriff of the county and was remembered locally with opprobrium as the 'priest-hunter'. Power was responsible in 1712 for the arrest of Bishop Ambrose Madden of Clonfert whom some sources claim was martyred in the present Eyre Square in Galway. Local lore says that Madden told Power that when he returned to his home he would have enough to worry about. When Power returned, he found his wife and servants in a state of great distress. His only son, a small child, had wandered from the house to fetch water from the lake and drowned. Local belief also holds that in his final days, Power himself went blind. Writing to Clanricarde in 1868, Bishop Derry confirms this belief by noting drily 'the visible punishment that befell Mr Power is traditionally well known'. In the early 1930s, however, an t-Athair Eric MacFhinn interviewed a man whose mother had spoken to a very old lady who had been a servant to the Power family. Her recollection was that Power was only blind in one eye. This old lady confirmed the lore about the death of Power's son and spoke of the family seat as 'a thatched house … with wings'. (Courtesy of Theo Hanley)

The eviction of Martin Ward, Church Street. (Courtesy of Clonfert Diocesan Archives)

Kennedy's shop on Bride Street. (Courtesy of Angela Bane)

Cosgrave's shop on Bride Street. (Courtesy of Angela Bane)

Looking up Main Street, early 1930s. To the left is Andrew Moeran's shop. He was considered one of the most successful businessmen in Galway at one time and the shop had a canopy that draped itself about ten feet over the shop front. It is now gone and marks the entrance to a car park. To the right of Moeran's was Sam Browne's boarding house. On one occasion Erma Waite, a 33-stone circus performer, stayed there and people were charged 3d to come and marvel at her size. Unfortunately, she fell ill and part of the frontage had to be demolished to get her out. Right of view, and marked by the fanlight over the door, was Johnny Foster's 'huckster' shop. (Courtesy of Clonfert Diocesan Archives)

From the early 1930s. The West Bridge with Cooney's house to the left and Morrissey's to the right. Centre-view is the entrance to Cabbage Lane or Dolphin Street. (Courtesy of Clonfert Diocesan Archives)

The Church of Ireland and Related Matters

The *Church of Ireland Gazette* from the earlier years of the twentieth century opens a window on an important part of the history of Loughrea and one of the most attractive buildings in the town is surely the library, which was built in 1821 for Protestant worship. In its early days it had pews designated for particular families and one family had their pew screened from view with scarlet curtains. Lighting was supplied with a tallow candle fixed in a tin sconce at the end of each pew. Such was the miserable nature of the tallow that the sexton, Mary Conway, was obliged to disport herself about the church midway in the service to replenish the candles. The poor box, made of copper and akin to a warming pan, was passed just prior to the sermon and the dropping of coins usually made an unholy racket. For charity sermons, the collection box was of silver. The pulpit stood under the east window.

In 1832 the spire was utterly destroyed by a bolt of lightning with a section falling through the roof and into the aisle. Fortunately, no service was being held at the time. For the duration of repairs, services were taken in the lecture room which was part of the school buildings once in Pigott's Lane. A comic incident, which caused much consternation at the time, concerns the sexton's lending of the communion table to an adjacent public house during an especially busy market day. There being no organ in the early days, harmony became a moot point but on one occasion any deficiency was lustily supplied by a visiting brigade of fusiliers under the command of Captain Sir William Russell (this must surely be Sir William Congreve Russell of the Worcestershires who later became an MP). In the 1820s the number of Protestants in Loughrea stood at 144, but by 1901 it had fallen to just 69. Some former congregants were Mrs Lloyd, the widow of a supervisor of excise and her three daughters and two sons. One daughter was to marry a Mr Moses Boodle from Liverpool. A son, George, took Holy Orders and ministered in the village of Croft, near Darlington in County Durham. Yet another worshipper was Mrs Paisley, who sang beautifully. She was a friend of Thomas Moore and a party piece of hers, which apparently left her audience howling with laughter, was to re-enact Moore's meeting with George IV who peremptorily marched off upon learning of the former's humble origins (you probably had to be there at the time). She owned a flour mill in Monasterevin which she leased to a Mr Cassidy. Mrs Paisley was to die near the town of Roscommon where a daughter had married one Mr Cullen. Her husband, William Dudley Fitzgerald Paisley, had preceded her in 1827.

Guy Newcome Ricard Armstrong was a well-known figure with a large family and had a bakery, worked various farms and was local postmaster. He was the first to establish a local loan office. He had a large number of dependents including his mother, three sons and a daughter not to mention a maiden sister, widowed cousin, her daughter and a male cousin. A Christian man, he even took in four orphans. He died in 1859 aged 68.

Mr Edmond Silk was holder of the title seneschal to the Marquis of Clanricarde, in essence his house steward and majordomo. By the mid-nineteenth century, however, his duties had ceased as Clanricarde no longer held Loughrea as his chief residence. Silk married Letitia Eyre who was descended from Colonel Stratford Eyre, Governor of Galway in the eighteenth century. He respectfully named his sons Stratford and Eyre. Silk died in 1846. Some of the congregants in the earlier part of the nineteenth century were comprised of army officers who had retired from the excitement of the Napoleonic Wars and the 'near-run thing' that was Waterloo. There were two Pigott's, one of whom gave his name to Pigott's Lane. Others included Rathbone, Tubbs, Bolger and Steele. A rank-and-file man called Johnny Rodney returned from the Peninsular Wars (minus one finger) and settled into mending pots and pans to earn a crust. Ballinasloe town had a similar story with an area called Waterloo Place, occupied by retired veterans. It was in May of 1862 that the streets of Loughrea were first lit with oil lamps.

Cabbage Lane was so-named because of the cabbage plants that were grown and sold there. It is now Dolphin Street. It was at a hedge school in Cabbage Lane that Séamus O'Kelly, the noted poet and writer, was educated.

Bróg-maker Lane acquired its name from the number of cobblers domiciled there and is now Moore Street.

Scallop Lane was to the rear of the fire station and was known for selling the scallops necessary for thatching roofs. Scallops were generally made of hazel and supple in order to secure the thatch to the roof.

Mount Carmel Crescent was known as Nunnery Lane and the Hill was Weaver's Lane. Barrack Street was Peter O'Finnerty Street in honour of a United Irishman who was a native of the town.

Donnellan Drive is named in honour of Brendan Donnellan who died fighting in the 1916 Rising. Aged 18, Donnellan joined the Volunteers while working in Gorevan's Drapery in Camden Street and was attached to 'E' company, 4th Battalion, under the command of Eamon Ceannt. He had been one of fifteen men assigned to the East Wall by Cathal Brugha to defend the eastern approaches and after withdrawing to Rialto Gate, was caught in sniper fire and killed. He is interred in Glasnevin Cemetery.

St Brendan's Cathedral now occupies a site which once played host to a row of thatched tenements and Monahan's Hotel (also known as the Head Inn), frequented by the Anglo-Irish novelist Charles Lever who wrote satirical novels. The tenements housed a few families each. It was also the location of the Posting House, a three-storied building which served as a departure point for travellers in horse-drawn transport. These were all demolished with a huge battering ram to make way for the building of the cathedral.

All these places have now vanished from Loughrea, swept into oblivion by the harsh winds of passing time and with them the knowledge of other places such as Gallow's Hill (at the end of Abbey Lane and where criminals were publicly executed), which now plays host to Mount Carmel Convent. Though a large body of infantry and constabulary were sited in Loughrea at the time, the most taxing duty was the sporadic seizure of an illegal poitín still or the forced reminder to an errant citizen of his duty to pay his tithe to the established church.

The Charter House

Charter schools were established in response to a suggestion made by Archbishop Hugh Boulter (1672–1742) of Armagh. The charter schools were an attempt to kill the Irish culture with kindness, a slow destruction through education. Through a charter granted in 1733, students would be fed, boarded and taught, commensurate with their station as colonised subjects. The Loughrea Charter School was begun at an uncertain date but was in existence by at least 3 April 1788 when the Hon. John Howard visited the establishment and found shocking conditions. Howard was a devoted Calvinist and a reformer and discovered that in many of the places he visited, the children were treated little better than slave labour. Furthermore, some highly dubious persons were in charge of the establishments, individuals more akin to the infamous Wackford Squeers of *Nicholas Nickleby* than to enlightened educators. In describing these wardens of education, Dickens called them: '... ignorant, sordid, brutal men, to whom few considerate persons would have entrusted the board

Hannah Barrett, daughter of Matty Coyne, with her children, from left to right: Matty, Sonny (James), Paddy, Joe and Kathleen. (Courtesy of Oliver Barrett)

and lodging of a horse or dog ...' John Howard would note of the Loughrea
Charter House that:

> It had ... 40 girls. These dirty, sickly objects without shoes and stockings
> were spinning and knitting in a cold room paved with pebbles. The usher
> stood, as at some other schools, with a rod in his hand to see the children
> work, but there was not a book to be seen. There were only 16 beds; sheets
> much wanted; the infirmary and potato house. The children were sadly
> neglected by their drunken mistress, but I observed that her own children
> by the fireside were fresh and clean.

Howard also describes a girl of 10 blowing on the fingers of an infant sister
to keep her warm; he also noted broken windows and filthy beds. A further
report of 1 February 1808 led to the school being suppressed as it was out of
repair. Thereafter, the school moved to a premises at Pigott's Lane. Howard
summed up the feeling of many compassionate Catholics and Protestants

Cllr Pat Hynes, Archbishop Giuseppe Lazzarotto (Nuncio to Ireland) and Mayor of Loughrea,
Anna Cronin at the celebrations to mark the centenary of St Brendan's Cathedral, October
2003. (Courtesy of Clonfert Diocesan Archives)

Fr Thomas Kennedy (1925–2006), a native of Loughrea and Msgr Thomas Matthews
who came from Killimor. Taken outside St Genevieve's church, Los Angeles in April 1951.
(Author's Private Archive)

A cup fit for kings … Fr Michael Finneran CC holding the McCarthy Cup with, from left
to right, Fr Iggy Clarke CC, Fr Ned Stankard CA and Fr TJ O'Connell CC, January 1981.
(Courtesy of Clonfert Diocesan Archives)

Rus-in-Urbe, Garrybreeda, which for a time was the home of St Brendan's College.
(Courtesy of Clonfert Diocesan Archives)

Msgr Bernard Bowes (1967–1960) in trademark homburg. Born in Main Street, Loughrea, he served the diocese for sixty-eight years and was parish priest of Tynagh 1919–1960. (Courtesy of Clonfert Diocesan Archives)

Mrs Chris Kilboy. (Courtesy of Sean Cleary)

when he wrote that the schools were 'dens of religious and mental ignorance and of moral and physical degradation … a disgrace to society'.

The Chicken and Cauliflower Duel

It is said that Ulick de Burgh, the 1st Marquess of Clanrickarde, was witness in the 1850s to a duel which took place in a hotel room in Loughrea and spoiled the dinner of a young subaltern/junior officer. Said subaltern had come to that town for the Knockbarron Races and was sitting down in his room to a repast of chicken and boiled cauliflower. In the room directly below him, a row had broken out and a pistol shot was discharged. After a short silence a second shot was fired with the result that the bullet came up through the floor and table, strewing the contents of the subaltern's dish in all directions. A tottering waiter hurried into the room and declared 'Don't be alarmed Captain! Councillor Burke has received Mr Keogh's shot and in the handsomest manner possible had fired in the air.' Spying the ashen-faced subaltern's dinner, the waiter added: 'But, bedad, he destroyed the cauliflower!' The last duel in England was fought in 1852 but one suspects the Irish kept the tradition running for a little longer.

Making a Mark Abroad

Natives of the diocese have left their imprint on civic life in all quarters of the world and one such individual was James Madden of Loughrea after whom Madden Street in Melbourne is named. A barrister by profession, he emigrated to Port Phillip and worked as a State school teacher at the Margaret Street seminary, latterly St Francis Xavier's, Launceston. He built the Formby Hotel in Devonport (which is in business to this day) at a time when West Formby was virgin territory. James Madden died at the house he built in Ulverstone in Tasmania, but not before leaving a little bit of Loughrea in Australia. We also note mention in old newspapers of the Loughrea Hotel on Elgin Street of Melbourne but it seems to be no longer extant. Yet another Loughrea native who lent his name to a civic area was Henry O'Neill who was born in 1799 and served in the Federal Army with the 28th Regiment of the Kentucky Volunteers. Married three times, he died shortly after becoming a father in his ninety-ninth year. O'Neill's Alley in Kentucky is named after him.

Reggie Bowes (1916–1941)

One of the current writer's great and much-lamented friends was Bertie Donohoe, who wrote for many years for the *Connacht Tribune* under the pen-name J.B.D. Bertie never failed to recall, on a frequent basis, his fallen fellow native and Garballian, Reggie Bowes, whose parents, Thomas and Margaret, had a business on Main Street (beside the current AIB). While a student at Garbally Park, he took part in the college operas, his most noted role being that of the Lady Saphir in the rarely performed Gilbert and Sullivan opera *Patience*. His brother played the title role and the newspaper critique stated that Reggie got 'due meed' for his performance. He is primarily remembered, however, as an outstanding rugby wing-forward and in a memorable match between Lansdowne and Garbally

Revd Dr Kevin Egan showing the Killoran statues to Dr Philbin, unknown dignatory and Fr Hycie O'Callaghan at the opening of the Clonfert Diocesan Museum, May 1957. (Courtesy of Clonfert Diocesan Archives)

Townspeople gather for opening of the Clonfert Diocesan Museum, May 1957. (Courtesy of Clonfert Diocesan Archives)

Leitrim Drum and Pipe Band march
through Loughrea, c. 1930. (Courtesy of
Pat Barrett)

Paddy Smith (1914–2000) with his wife Evelyn at his investiture in 1989 as a Knight of
the Order of St Sylvester. This honour has been bestowed by the Holy See on only a few
Irishmen, including the late Frank Patterson and Liam Cosgrave. (Courtesy of Pat Smith)

Dr William Philbin speaking at the opening of the Clonfert Diocesan Museum, May 1957.
Clergy to the rear are, from left to right: Revd Pat Bruen, Vinnie Marren and John Fahy.
(Courtesy of Clonfert Diocesan Archives)

Houses on Cabbage Lane, now Dolphin Street. (Courtesy of Pat Barrett)

in 1934, converted Garbally's three tries and added two penalty goals, Garbally winning 21-15. He went on to study medicine at UCG and was a member there of the Senior Rugby XV which won the Connacht Senior Cup on two occasions and the Connacht Senior league on three. There was great dismay in Loughrea and the surrounding districts when the *Connacht Tribune* announced on 4 October 1941, 'Connacht Rugby Star Missing'. He had joined the Royal Air Force Volunteer Reserve, was promoted to sergeant (Service No. 989280) and was one of a crew of five (he as observer/navigator) who took off from RAF base Topline at 21.01 on 29 August 1941. The plane went missing, presumed shot down, over Frankfurt-on-Oder. He was aged only 25. Reggie Bowes and his fellow crew members are interred at the Rheinberg War Cemetery in Nordrhein-Westfal, some 85 kilometres north of Koln, among a total of 3,326 other Commonwealth servicemen, mostly Royal Air Force.

Major-Surgeon Denis P. O'Farrell outside his house on Bride Street, Loughrea, c. 1910. This is the house opposite what is now Maggie May's. His son, Professor Thomas O'Farrell, recorded extracts from the censi of 1821 and 1841 for Loughrea prior to the bombardment of the Four Courts. (Courtesy of Pat Barrett)

Fr Myles Gannon (1781–1864)

Most biographies of the town of Loughrea focus on luminaries like Edward Martyn and Bishop Healy but a somewhat overlooked figure is surely Fr Myles. Born in Ahascragh to Dennis and Isabel (*née* Ryan) Gannon, he was professed at Sargossa, Spain on 15 May 1806. Ordained in 1810, he returned to Ireland on 6 August of the same year. Fr James P. Rushe in his *The Abbey, Loughrea* and Fr Phelim Monahan in his *History of the Discalced Carmelites in Loughrea* give interesting detail on his life and work. The abbey was in a lamentable state when he returned to his native county. He set about rebuilding the chapel which was duly consecrated by Dr Coen in 1820. He also set his mind to building a new conventual residence at a cost of £3,500. To this project he personally invested almost £1,500 which was his thorough inheritance. On the named Gallows Hill he built Mount Carmel for the sisters. While all this work was apace, he engaged in pastoral work in the town of Loughrea.

We are fortunate that, unlike so many others, he recorded in the annals of the abbey the task ahead. He wrote:

> We deem it necessary to leave something authentic from under my hand, showing the condition of this Convent at the period of my arrival here from Spain in 1810 ... I came to Loughrea Convent, accompanied by the Rev Fr Hyland, and Rev Fr John Reilly. At this time the convent was in a very impoverished state, and the House without any means of support; without convenience or furniture, of even the poorest description. The Chapel was a wretched building, small and confined, in a state of dilapidation, and in danger of falling any day on the heads of the Congregation. The Convent House was also small, narrow, and insecure, composed of bad materials, and dangerous to inhabit.

He died on Friday 22 April 1864.

Pope Emeritus Benedict XVI meets Bishop John Kirby. (Courtesy of Clonfert Diocesan Archives)

Dr Joseph Cassidy, Bishop of Clonfert 1983–1988 greets Garret Fitzgerald at the New Ireland Forum 1984. (Courtesy of Tuam Diocesan Archives)

John Dignan, Bishop of Clonfert 1924–1953, who commissioned Revd Patrick K. Egan to conduct a photographic survey of the diocese. (Courtesy of Clonfert Diocesan Archives)

Dr William Philbin, Bishop of Clonfert 1954–1962. (Courtesy of Clonfert Diocesan Archives)

Bishop William Philbin, clergy and religious process down Barrack Street on the occasion of Fr Peyton's Rosary Rally on 16 May 1954. Up to 15,000 people thronged the town. (Courtesy of Pat Barrett)

Bishop Thomas Ryan
celebrates outdoor Mass
at St Brendan's Cathedral.
(Courtesy of Pat Barrett)

Pat Barrett, Loughrea native and raconteur *par excellence*. (Courtesy of Pat Barrett)

A New Genealogical Source

Among the many casualties of the 1922 Civil War was the heritage of the country when landmines were set off in the Public Records Office of the Four Courts. Fortunately, the late Professor Thomas O'Farrell, who had strong family links with Loughrea, recorded some snippets from the 1821 and 1841 Censi of Loughrea town. His notes, which were typed manually, are presented here in full and may be of some use for those bridging genealogical gaps. There are difficulties in that O'Farrell only provided a portion of the returns and seems to have excluded those he felt were unimportant; he also provides no key as to what building fits which return. Nonetheless, he could never have foreseen the destruction that the Civil War was to wreak and in the genealogy business, one takes what one can find. There are some misspellings in the text. As it is impossible to determine whether these were mistakes on the part of Dr O'Farrell or the census enumerator, they have been left as are, with a *sic erat scriptum*. The returns for the Galway Road have something of a poignancy about them when one considers that many of these houses were destroyed by the fire that swept through this district of Loughrea after the Night of the Big Wind on 6 January 1839. Given the limits of medical science at the time, the shadow of death hovers over some of the returns. The cholera outbreak of 1832 is especially noted. The 1841 Census contains some more detailed information and when compared with parochial records may lead some to tie down a relation.

Census of 1821

No of House	No of Stories	Name	Age	Occupation
Market St				
24	2	Michael Madden	40	Shoemaker
		Sarah Madden	20	Wife
46	3	William O'Farrell	31	Apothecary
		Park [*sic*] Staunton	15	Apprentice
		Mary Daly	60	House Servant
		James Cuthbertson	30	Visitor

78	2	Thomas Walsh	28	Attorney
		Honora	26	Wife
		Daniel	5	Son
		Thomas	4	Son
		Bridget Carr	27	House Servant
89		Peter Bolton Richardson	25	Printer (occasionally employed)
		Sharlotte [sic]	23	Wife
		Margaret	1¼	Daughter
		Elenor [sic] Daly	22	House Servant
102	3	John Daly	28	
		Michael O'Farrell	3	Nephew
		Thomas O'Farrell	4	Nephew
		Bridget Egan	60	Inhabitant
		William Colgan	14	Apprentice
		Honora Mahounan [sic]	26	House Servant
		Mary McCar	20	House Servant
		Honora Staunton	14	House Servant
Barrack St				
22	3	Thomas Shadwell	30	Doctor
		Elener [sic]	36?	Wife
		George	8	Son
		Mary Fahy	20	House Servant
		Honora Dempsey	20	House Servant
Kelly's Lane				
5	2	Martin Winter	50	Farmer
		Catherine	50	Wife
		Peter	22	Son
		John	15	Son
		Margaret	16	Daughter
		John Martin	4½	Grandson
		Catherine Robins [sic]	24	Lodger
Abbey Lane				

11			Patrick Daly	40	Coach-Maker
			Belle	23	Wife
			John	Under 1	Son
15			Thomas Daly	27	Brogue-Maker (occasionally employed)
			Catherine	24	Wife
			Thomas	3½	Son
			Bridget	1½	Daughter
Church Lane					
1	2		Arthur Henry Daly	50	No profession listed
			Charlotte	28	Wife
			Arthur Ag. [sic]	21	Son
			Michael J.	18	Son
			Denis B.	15	Son
			Hyacinth Thos G.	11	Son
			Charles	9	Son
			Isabella Jane	19	Daughter
			Letitia B.	16	Daughter
			Anne	4	Daughter
			Charlotte	1	Daughter
			James Madden	18	House Servant
			Margaret Madden	26	House Servant
			Bridget Madden	26	House Servant
Abbey Lane					
51			Patrick Farrell	70	No profession listed
			Catherine	50	Sister
			Anne	60	Sister
			Judith	60	Sister
65			Mathew Daly	26	Tailor
			Elenor [sic]	25	Wife
			Anne	4	Daughter

		Eliza	2	Daughter
		Michael Burke	19	Apprentice
		Thady Hoban	22	Lodger
		Honour Bards [*sic*]	18	House Servant
		And 3 lodgers		
Athenry Rd				
62		Thomas Walsh	50	No profession listed
		Anne Walsh	40	Wife
		Richard Walsh	18	Son
		Biddy	12	Daughter
		Mary	9	Daughter
Galway Rd				
17		James Wall	34	Weaver
		Eliz Walsh [*sic*]	40	Wife
		Steohen [*sic*]Walsh	13	Son
		Thomas Walsh	7	Son
		Mary Walsh	Under 1	Daughter
36		Andrew Bryan	60	Farmer and Stonecutter
		Mary	60	Wife
		Belinda	23	Daughter
		Margaret	20	Daughter
		Bridget	18	Daughter
		Honora	16	Daughter
		Anne Egan	7	Granddaughter
		Bridget Walsh	11	Granddaughter
		Thomas Walsh	5	Grandson
64		Patrick Daly	80	No profession listed
		Margaret	50	Wife
		Cecilia	24	Daughter
		William	26	Son
		Mary Tarpy	1 ¾	Granddaughter

78		Laurence Farrell	50	No profession listed
		Winny	50	Wife
		Thomas	10	Son
		James	8	Son
99		Martin Walsh	43	Weaver
		Bridget	40	Wife
		Mary	13	Daughter
		Teresa	10	Daughter
		Martin	80	Father, Weaver
147		Anne Walsh	38	Widow, Flax-spinner
		Stephen	13	Son
		Mary	11	Daughter
		Catherine	8	Daughter
179		Mary Farrell	30	Dealer
		Anne Kilkelly	7	Daughter
		Biddy Kilkelly	13	Daughter
210		Peter Daly	40	Skinner
		Eliza	40	Wife
		Eliza	10	Daughter
		Mary Deigh [sic]	27	House Servant
		Eliz Charleton	24	Lodger
Bride St				
55		Michael Daly	36	No profession listed
		Catherine	33	Wife
		John	11	Son
		Patrick	9	Son
		Edmund	4	Son
		Biddy	6	Daughter
		Mary	13	Daughter
		Anne	Under 1	Daughter

57		Patrick Daly	40	No profession listed
		Catherine	30	Wife
		Fanny	7	Daughter
		Joseph	5	Son
		Mary Hogan	12	Niece-in-law
79		William Farrell	40	¼ Acre
		Honora	36	Wife
		Thomas	12	Son
		Michael	10	Son
		John	5	Son
		Anthony	4	Son
		Judy	70	Mother
Boherbuoy [sic]		Thomas Daly	43	No profession listed
		Mary	40	Wife
		Thomas	15	Son
Shrahaunacrusha				
11	2	William Winter	55	Tanner
		Anne		Wife
		William	27	Son
		Michael	23	Son
		Henry	13	Son
		Anne	14	Daughter
		Celia	12	Daughter
		Honor Carenan? (next to school house)	23	House Servant
Mount Pleasant				
1		John Daly	60	No profession listed
		Dominic	59	Brother
		Johanna	40	Sister-in-law
		Malachy	26	Nephew
		Thomas	25	Son
		Dominic	24	Nephew

		Louisa	27	Niece
		Marcella	23	Niece
		Anne	22	Niece
		Johanna	20	Niece
		Richard Skerret	45	Butler
		Michael Kelly	26	Groom
		Margaret Winne [sic]	23	Cook
		Cecilia Augagan [sic]	30	House Servant
		Mgt Burke	35	Kitchen Servant
		Anne Davin	24	Child Maid
Mount Vene present name for monuments		*Author's Note: This is not explained in Dr O'Farrell's text		
		John Farrell	60	Labourer
		Eleanor	50	Wife
		Peter	18	Son
		Eleanor	17	Daughter
		Bridget	15	Daughter
		Catherine	13	Daughter
		Margaret	10	Daughter
		Catherine Murray	47	Lodger, Pauper

1841 Census

Address	Name	Age	Comments
Main St			
	Edward Hyor	30	Bank Manager (of Waterford)
	Margaret	21	Wife (of Galway)
	Edward	8 mths	Son
	Anne Feeny	32	Servant
	Bridget Staunton	21	Nurse
	Augustine Coyne	40	Bank Porter
	Laurence Fahy	46	Married 1817

	Belinda	51	Wife (married 1817 and also 1801)
	Maria	20	
	Honoria	35	
	Laurence	26	
	Stephen Madden	56	Commissioner of affidavits
	Honoria	52	Wife
	James Darcy	24	Son
	Mary Matilda	22	Daughter
	Sarah	21	Daughter
	Isabella Daly	36	Married 1823
	Peter	16	Son
	Mary Anne	14	Daughter
	Matilda	13	Daughter
	Margaret	10	Daughter
	John	7	Son
	John Daly	40	Husband, Absent, in America
	Belinda	17	Daughter, Absent, at school in Galway
	Mary Daly	53	Married 1816–1824 Dealer
	Bridget	15	Daughter
	Michael Egan	41	Malster
	Clare	32	Wife
	Julia	9	Daughter
	Mary	7	Daughter
	Patrick	2	Son
	Honoria	1 mth	Daughter
	Pat Egan	5	Away

	Julia Egan		Mother of, Died of cholera in 1832 aged 63
	Matthew Egan		Brother of, Died of cholera in 1832 aged 34
	Patrick Egan		Father of, Farmer, Died of weakness in 1841
Bohercom Lane			
	Mathias Coin	50	Fisherman, Married 1817
	Bridget	40	Wife
	Pat	23	Son
	William	14	Son
Bride St			
	Henry Cloran	29	Medical doctor, Married 1835, from Loughrea
	Eleanor	32	Wife, born in Dublin
	Henry	3 yrs 8 mths	Son, born in Dublin
	John	11 mths	Son, born Loughrea
	Thomas Byrne	30	Servant, Married 1837
	Ella Moriarity	23	
	Anne Kelly	19	
	Joseph Farrell	23	
Dunkellin St			
	Thomas Walsh	49	Solicitor & Attorney for Galway
	Agnes	36	Wife
	Mary Frances	21	Daughter
	William John	16	Son, Studies
	Honoria	8 yrs, 11 mths	Daughter, School
	Ellen	5 yrs, 10 mths	Daughter
	Agnes Grace Eliz	4 mths	
	Charles	8 mths	
	Stephen Madden	29	Brother-in-law, Gentleman at large

	7 Servants & 2 nurses		
	Thomas Walsh	23 yrs, 2 mths	Away, Son, Attorney
	Ellen Walsh	30	Away, Sister, Gort
	Daniel	24	Away, Son, East India Co, Serving Shelpore, India
	Honoria Walsh		First wife, Died aged 40 in 1832
	Frances Walsh	1 yr, 10 mths	Daughter, died in 1841 of croup

Bishop William Philbin on the occasion of his consecration as Bishop of Clonfert Sunday 14 March 1954, flanked by, from left to right: Msgr Richard Callanan, Fr James Cogavin and Fr Hycie O'Callaghan. (Courtesy of Pat Barrett)

Following Dr Philbin's consecration with President Séan T. O'Ceallaigh and Taoiseach Eamon de Valera. (Courtesy of Pat Barrett)

Dr Joseph Cassidy greets crowds outside St Brendan's Cathedral, Loughrea following his consecration as Coadjutor Bishop of Clonfert on 23 September 1979. (Courtesy of Michael Donohoe)

A prince of the Church … an exuberant Richard Cardinal Cushing of New York waves to the crowd gathered on the occasion of his visit to Loughrea in May 1965. He told the people, 'I came from the poor and I like the poor.' Cushing's father, who was born in County Cork, was a blacksmith. He is flanked by Fr Dermot Byrne (left) and Fr William Cummins (right). (Courtesy of Pat Barrett)

A fallen leader … Archbishop Joseph Walsh of Tuam leads mourners in prayer at the grave of Bishop John Dignan, 15 April 1953. (Courtesy of Pat Barrett)

3

LEITRIM AND
KILMEEN

Situated between Loughrea and Woodford, this parish is an honourable eccentricity in the diocese as it contains the only 'island' parish in Clonfert, Kilmeen, which has been part of the archdiocese of Tuam since the Synod of Kells in AD 1152.

Fr Martin Charles O'Farrell. Born at Ballymanagh House, Craughwell on 23 December 1879, he was ordained from Maynooth in 1906 where two classmates were Fr Richard Callanan and Fr John Madden. Known affectionately to his colleagues as 'Cha'. CC Leitrim 1906–1910, CC Tynagh 1910–1912, CC Killimor 1912–1916 (where he built the old curate's residence), CC Eyrecourt 1916–1917, CC Ballinakill 1917–1920, CC Kilrickle 1920–1926 (where he built the school). He died 2 May 1942 and is interred in the grounds of St Andrew's church, Leitrim. He had an especially difficult station in Kilrickle where he was persecuted by the local RIC on account of his nationalist views and strong preaching. A brother, Fr Joseph, was a priest of Galway diocese and died in 1967. Fr Martin was a hugely popular parish priest in Leitrim and in 1933 he wrote of the lot of the Irish farmer, saying: '1932 was the most unprosperous year the Irish farmers ever experienced. Plenty of food – but no money for stock. Many others, through no fault of their own are down and out. Were it not for the spiritual graces given them during Congress Week many of them would have given up hope.' (Courtesy of Eithne Whiriskey)

Revd Edward Doran, CA 1933–1935. A native of Cappoquin, County Waterford, his father was postmaster in Ballinasloe and latterly Dun Laoighaire. Ordained 1921 at the Pines College Chapel, Ballinasloe, he served in Los Angeles for almost ten years before becoming CA Leitrim when Fr O'Farrell fell ill. A man with a delicate constitution, his neighbour Laurence Smyth often shot pigeons for Fr Doran's housekeeper to make pigeon soup which it was believed was good for bronchitis. Died 21 April 1935 and interred in the precincts of St Andrew's church, Leitrim. (Author's Private Archive)

Éamonn Ó Dcórain, Cluain Fcarta

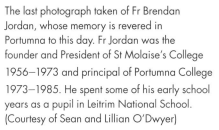

The last photograph taken of Fr Brendan Jordan, whose memory is revered in Portumna to this day. Fr Jordan was the founder and President of St Molaise's College 1956–1973 and principal of Portumna College 1973–1985. He spent some of his early school years as a pupil in Leitrim National School. (Courtesy of Sean and Lillian O'Dwyer)

Fr Martin Leahy (1859–1944) a native of Killeen townland and parish priest of Eyrecourt, Clonfert and Meelick 1898–1944. He was CA Loughrea when the foundation stone was laid for the cathedral. (Courtesy of Clonfert Diocesan Archives)

Bullaun and Rath

The ancient bullaun of Leitrim is at present located just south of Leitrim Fort, near a hedgerow on the west side of a field. Cut in granite, it is said to have been used in druidical rites but was later appropriated by the earliest Christians in the area as a baptismal font. Local tradition holds that up to 3,000 were baptised with its water. Up until the mid-twentieth century, people used it for superstitious reasons, applying its waters to warts and sores while reciting the words 'Water of a rock, without seeking you I found you as I came the way'. The landowner is Mr Hugh Joe Fahy, a sprightly 94-year-old, who recalls a time the stone stood on a cairn in the middle of the field. It is possible that Christianity had its origins in the parish at this very spot and perhaps the local pagan chieftain was baptised here. The townland of Masonbrook hosts one of the finest extant examples of a rath, often referred to as the 'Palace of the King of Loughrea and Leitrim'. The soutterain therein is immaculately preserved. The rath may have been plundered by the Norsemen led by Turgesius when

The writer and 94-year-old Hugh Joe Fahy discuss the Leitrim bullaun. (Courtesy of Dr Christy Cunniffe)

they raided Loughrea in AD 843 and was possibly occupied by them latterly. Southerrains are still something of an archaeological bone of contention. Manmade tunnels, they are considered to have been places of refuge when danger threatened though recent scholarship holds that the more simply constructed ones were for storing victuals.

It is unknown when the first Christians came to the area, but it is peppered with the remains of ecclesiastical sites. In Kilcooley townland, on a prominent height, stands the remains of a church containing a vaulted chamber which is the final resting place of the Kellys of Coolaney. The oldest headstone in the adjoining cemetery is dated 'AD 1780' and has a Latin inscription, which is unusual for the time. This headstone bears striking similarity in style and motif to the gravestone of Ned Mullen, a hermit and sculptor who resided in the neighbouring parish of Ballinakill, and may have been carved by him. Around the outer precincts of the cemetery are several tiny enclosures with stones embedded in their embankments. From a distance they appear as small gardens, indicating a *clachán cille* which may have been occupied by a small estate of workers in nearby Kilcooley Castle, once the residence of Norah Óge Burke of the Clanrickard dynasty. Reportedly a place of formidable strength, tradition says that passers-by who refused to remove their caps were fired upon. Another story holds that Patrick Sarsfield used this spot as one of his many stops en route to Limerick from Aughrim. Kilcooley Cemetery and the castle were once linked by a road, the cobbles of which are still discernible beneath the grassy fields between.

A church of more venerable vintage is Kilteskill or the 'church of the Gospel'. A former bishop of Clonfert is believed to be buried here but his name is unknown. Few burials now take place there.

The medieval church in Leitrim Mór was erected by the de Burgos of Leitrim Castle, but was destroyed in 1583 when the castle fell following the murder of John de Burgo, Baron of Leitrim, at a banquet hosted by his own brother. Yet another version of the story has the murder take place at Ballyfintan Castle in Mullagh parish. The present parish church was built between 1856 and 1858 by Fr Andrew Griffin, a native of Ballyfa, New Inn. An energetic man, such were the times in which he lived, that he was obliged to carry about a walking stick in which was secreted a sabre. The ringfort on Pat and Mary Smyth's land in Killeen townland was also the place of refuge for Fr (later Bishop) John Dignan when the Black and Tans were intent upon murdering him in 1921.

Suited and booted. Revd Dr John O'Connor, parish priest of Leitrim, making his way to the confirmation ceremony at St Brendan's church, Mullagh, 8 June 1943. The trusty Ford Prefect can be seen right. (Courtesy of Clonfert Diocesan Archives)

Leitrim Drum and Pipe Band marching through Kylebrack in June 1937. (Courtesy of Paddy Larkin)

Fr Vincent Finnerty ODC (1860–1931).
A native of Leitrim Mills, he entered
the Carmelite Order in 1885 and
was ordained in Dublin in 1892
by Archbishop Walsh. He died at
Castlemartyr, County Cork and is
interred at the Abbey, Loughrea.
A window in St Andrew's church,
Leitrim, is dedicated to his memory.
(Courtesy of Mary Finnerty)

Leitrim bullaun. (Courtesy of Dr Christy Cunniffe)

Taking a well-earned rest – Fr Thomas J. Kennedy receives a presentation from parishioners on his retirement, September 2005. (Courtesy of Paddy Larkin)

More relaxed clerical days at Leitrim parochial house with Fr M.C. O'Farrell and Fr John Sellars, parish priest. The house, here seen enshrouded in Boston ivy, had been built in 1886 and was demolished in April 2008. It was one of the last remaining parish houses to contain a garret, or attic-room for the housekeeper. Such spaces were a spatial statement about social-status as they were not seen as rooms-proper and thus may be regarded as architecturally liminal spaces. Such a view was testified to by John Dubois (1764–1842), a much put-upon bishop of New York. Dubois was French and despite being a dedicated and sincere cleric, was constantly being downed by the lay trustees of his cathedral. During one dispute, they threatened to withhold his salary, prompting a classical episcopal riposte. Dubois wrote to them: 'I am an old man and do not need much. I can live in a basement or in a garret. But, whether I come up from the basement or down from the garret, I shall still be your bishop'. (Courtesy of Leitrim/Kilmeen parish)

Bog-Butter

A relic of the ancient past to be found in local bogs was 'bog-butter' which was actually rendered sheep fat. In 1931, Fr Martin O'Farrell, parish priest, claimed that in the eighteenth century, rustled sheep would be stripped of their fat and then boiled down. This fat was then secreted in casks in the bog and used as dripping for dressing vegetables. As recently as 2011, such a find was unearthed in Ballard bog, Tullamore, County Offaly and was believed to be 5,000 years old.

The Well at Carrowkeel

In 1931, James O'Malley recited for Fr Martin C. O'Farrell, parish priest, the following poem entitled 'Lines on the Closing of Carrowkeel Well', composed by a local schoolteacher, Mr Francis Swift. O'Malley had received the poem from his own father some forty-five years before. The O'Carrolls of Carrowkeel House resented trespassers who were using the old Mass path that ran near the House (and who called to the well in question for cures) and so had it closed up. The O'Carrolls sent for Swift and demanded that he apologise for writing the poem but he refused and stated that he would not be surprised if the fate of Tantalus befell those responsible for the well's closure. Tantalus was a Greek mythological figure stricken with excessive thirst. Standing before a pool of cool water, the pool would draw away whenever he bent down for a drink and the luscious fruit tree above his head would withdraw from his grasp whenever he reached up to sate his hunger, hence the word *tantalise*. The clever Mr Swift wrote:

> This well to all I do appeal,
> Was once great use to Carrowkeel,
> Enclosed in, by its little bank,
> 'Tis the purest water e'er was drank,
> On Sunday when o'erpowered by heat,
> I sought this well which was no cheat,
> 'Twon't set me mad nor make me blind,
> Or make me leave my cash behind,
> Or make me hideous to view,
> As some spring wells are wont to do,
> And where waters oft doth pass,
> Through the chalice at the Holy Mass,

But some vile demon to me unknown,
Hath closed it up with fir and stone,
But through his mischief he has surely sought,
The punishment Tantalus got,

And Charon soon his sails will fix,
And sail him over the river Styx.

Swift managed to put the fear of God into the O'Carrolls and the well was hastily reopened.

Confirmation at Leitrim, 1984. From left to right: Mrs Mary Dolan NT, Mrs Tríona Kennedy NT, Bishop Joseph Cassidy, Fr John Hawkins PP, Mrs Alice McArdle NT, Mrs Carmel Flannery NT. (Courtesy of Jimmy Leahy)

A confirmation ceremony in progress at St Andrew's, May 1944. Dr Dignan is about to give the final benediction. The ceiling-timbers shown are the original ones from 1858 and by 1958 were sufficiently decayed to be replaced with roof-trusses which now come to the apex of the main sanctuary window. (Courtesy of Clonfert Diocesan Archives)

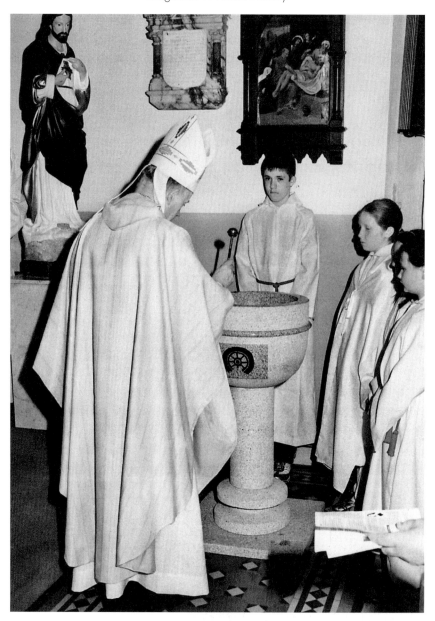

Archbishop Neary blesses the new baptism font at St Jarlath's on his visit to Ballydugan in May, 2007 with, from left to right: Gavin Treacy, Fiona Whelan and Anna Flynn. (Courtesy of Fergus Benson)

Bishop Kirby, assisted by Rt Revd Msgr Cathal Geraghty, consecrates the new altar at St Andrew's at the reopening ceremony on 30 November 2008. Composed of Barnacullia granite, it was created by renowned sculptor Tom Glendon and incorporates the saltyr or X-shaped cross on which St Andrew was reputedly crucified. (Courtesy of Theo Hanley)

Jack Kenny, Newtowndaly, obliges the photographer. Born in 1922 and still hale and hearty, Jack has seen twelve parish priests of Leitrim and five bishops of Clonfert. (Courtesy of Fergus Benson)

Kilmeen

Once a fruitful source of dissension between two bishops, Kilmeen bears evidence of having been the location of a high-status religious settlement. Tradition holds that there were once so many monks between Kilmeen, Kilcooley and Kilbocht that were they to stand hand-to-hand, there would be a sufficient number to encompass the distances between all three locations.

The ancient cemetery in Kilmeen contains what is believed to be the basal layer of a round-tower. According to archaeologist Roger Stalley, a general rule-of-thumb is that round-towers are twice their circumference in height. As Kilmeen has a circumference of 48 feet, it was possibly up to 100 feet high. Given that it is the only known contender as a round-tower in Clonfert, one might speculate that its attachment to Tuam made it a site of high status and thus the tower marked it as such. How the parish separated from Clonfert is uncertain but the belief is that the abbot there, at the time of the Synod of Kells, moved to Athenry and brought ownership of the lands with him. Annaghbride townland nearby suggests by the derivation of the name that a convent of nuns was located there and dedicated to St Brigid.

Dalyston

The principal landowners in Leitrim were the O'Farrell family. The O'Dalys were a Bardic Gaelic family who came to political power in Connacht after the Battle of the Boyne. Hyacinth Daly died in 1782 and was succeeded by his son, the Rt Hon Denis Bowes Daly, MP for County Galway. In 1780 he married Charlotte Ponsonby, daughter of Sir John Ponsonby, Speaker of the House of Commons in Ireland. Lady Charlotte's nephew was Major-General William Ponsonby who was killed in action while leading the Charge of the Scots Greys at the Battle of Waterloo. Bowes Daly disliked the fact that so many wretched little dwellings spoiled his view of the landscape and so he relocated many of the tenants from his estate to the townland of Kilmacrah 2 miles away, giving rise to the current townland name of Newtowndaly. His son got into financial difficulties at the time of the Famine and sold the estate to the O'Farrell family. Bowes Daly held to no religion, had no funeral service himself and such was his love for his wife that when she died only a year after their marriage, it was believed that he had her body embalmed, stored in the house for years and that both were buried together when he died forty-one years later. Such was the depth of his grief that after her death he refused to even leave the house for twelve months. Their tomb in Dalyston private cemetery bears an inscription from a line spoken by Prospero in Shakespeare's *The Tempest*: 'We are such stuff as dreams are made of, and our little life is rounded with a sleep.'

Local lore says that the embalmed Lady Charlotte was the inspiration for the story *Sleeping Beauty*. The boundaries of folklore are relatively fluid and this story proves as much. There is no evidence that either Jacob or Williem Grimm ever visited Ireland, let alone heard of Dalyston. The story of *Sleeping Beauty* was first published in 1697 by Charles Perrault and even then drew on a medieval romance story *Perceforest* dating to 1528. It does, however, make for a good yarn.

The story of the embalming, however, is true and was reported in *The Observer* in July 1832, eleven years after Bowes Daly had died. Shortly after his death, workmen found a secret closet in Dalyston House, a closet to which none but Bowes Daly himself had access. Therein was found his wife's body, 'in a high state of preservation'. Servants recalled their late master frequently visiting the chamber. The surprise was that at the time of her death, a funeral had taken place and a coffin had been interred in a specially built cenotaph in Dalyston private cemetery. Upon discovery, arrangements were obviously made to lay the lady to proper rest. It was also recalled how Bowes Daly always wore a locket around his neck, which a friend claimed contained the ashes of his late wife's heart.

Sr Mary Aidan Flynn (1914–2013) LSU, on the occasion of the centenary of St Brendan's Cathedral. At the time of her death, she was the oldest living native of the parish. (Courtesy of Eleanor Flynn)

Archbishop Neary blesses the congregation on the occasion of the first recorded visit of an Archbishop of Tuam to Kilmeen in May 2007. (Courtesy of Fergus Benson)

Confirmation ceremony, May 1944. Bishop Dignan is greeted by parishioners. (Courtesy of Clonfert Diocesan Archives)

Fr James Flynn (1865–1906), a native of Lisafooka and nephew of the renowned Fr Patrick Costello, parish priest of Woodford. A window to Fr Flynn's memory was erected in St Michael's church, Ballinasloe, by the Gaelic League after his death. He had been cycling with some colleagues to a concert in Banagher when one of his tyres punctured. He bade his colleagues go on while he pumped the wheel. After an undue delay, they returned to find him dying on the roadside. A local farmer had seen him hurrying to catch up and being thrown from the bicycle with such force that his injuries claimed his life. He is interred in the old cemetery at Leitrim medieval church. (Courtesy of Eleanor Flynn)

Fr Andrew Flynn (1877–1909), a brother of Fr James. Ordained in 1901, his ministry was a tragically short one as he suffered from pernicious anaemia and often required the assistance of his father when celebrating Mass. He died 4 February 1909 and was interred in the precincts of St Andrew's church, Leitrim. (Courtesy of Eleanor Flynn)

Fr Patrick Lyons (1811–1885), the formidable parish priest of Kilmeen. (Courtesy of Ciss Lyons)

Confirmandi with their teachers outside Leitrim Church, May 1944. (Courtesy of Clonfert Diocesan Archives)

The Battle of Ballydugan – 20 June 1652

It was during the course of a hard-fought campaign against the attempt to site an incinerator in the parish that this long-forgotten battle came to light. The information was supplied by Dr Padraig Lenihan, an eminent historian, who explained its significance at a ceremony to unveil a commemorative plaque near the site of the battle. On that occasion, Dr Lenihan said:

> Its real significance and importance lies in the fact that it was the last battle, not just in Ireland but in three kingdoms – Ireland, England and Scotland – against the Cromwellian Parliamentary forces.

Irish resistance leader Richard Grace had encamped in the vicinity of Loughrea when word came that a large detachment of Cromwellian forces were approaching from the south-east. Though Grace attempted to make good his escape, his troops were forced to engage the enemy in Ballydugan bog where several hundred Irish soldiers were slain. Some managed to flee through the bogs and the woods. Grace was captured but permitted to leave. Almost forty years later, he was one of the officers defending Athlone against the Williamite advance just prior to the Battle of Aughrim, warning that he would defend the town until forced to eat his own boots from starvation. Local resident Mr Tom Treacy told the current writer how his father-in-law, 85-year-old Mr Brendan Burke, recalled the older people in his childhood speaking of a prophecy of how the stream of Kilmeen would one day 'run red with blood'. This came from the *Prophecies of Colmcille*, a popular work published by Nicholas O'Kearney in 1856. It foretold that Kilmeen would run red with blood for twenty-four hours. But as Tom says himself, 'The old people got it back-to-front. They saw it as a future event whereas the local streams had already run red with blood on that fateful day 350 years ago.'

Interior of St Jarlath's, Ballydugan, 1944. (Courtesy of Clonfert Diocesan Archives)

Jack Forde of Hollyhill and his sister stand against the remnants of Norah-Óge's castle of Kilcooley, July 1937. This portion of the tower house was finally demolished in the mid-1960s as it had become dangerously unstable. (Courtesy of Jack Forde)

Mrs Bridgie Larkin receiving the Fr James Cullen Medal from Leitrim/Kilcooley PTAA on 8 December 2006. Standing, from left to right: John Dillon, Brendan Melody, Mary Horan, Michael Flynn, Bid Hedderman, Stephen Leahy, Marie Leahy, Padraig Forde, Kathleen Forde, Brian Fahy. Seated: Fr Declan Kelly CA, Mrs Bridgie Larkin, Ciss Lyons, Eleanor Flynn. The Fr Cullen Memorial Medal is awarded to Pioneers with long service. (Courtesy of Leitrim/Kilcooley PTAA)

Brendan O'Malley, Leitrim Mór and John T. Flanagan, Glanasloth, chat after the visit of Archbishop Neary to Ballydugan in May 2007. (Courtesy of Fergus Benson)

Sr Benedict Costello, a native of Leitrim Mór
and, at 97, the oldest living native of the
parish. (Courtesy of Mary Jo Costello)

Retirement of a teaching legend. Mrs Alice McArdle, one of the most-loved teachers in
the history of the parish, at her farewell presentation in late August 1982. She was the
third generation of teachers in her family and her maternal grandmother had been one of
the first pupils in the Convent of Mercy after its foundation in 1854, later teaching there.
Mrs McArdle died 15 July 2003. Back Row, from left to right: Stephen Dolan (RIP), Sadie
Coleman, Tommy Lowry, Sean Flannery, Tom Loughnane, Margaret Fahy. Middle Row:
Brendan Melody, Tony Molloy (RIP), Andy Flynn (RIP), Margaret Skelly, Alice McArdle (RIP),
Eileen Callanan, Sean Callanan, Pat Flanagan, Pakie Dolphin, Gerry Donohue. Front row:
Ina Molloy, Carmel Flannery, Ita lowry, Mary T. Dolan (RIP). (Courtesy of Mary T. Dolan)

Celebrating the reopening of
St Andrew's church, Leitrim,
30 November 2008. Cllr Gabriel
Burke and Paddy Larkin,
Chairman of the Pastoral Council.
(Courtesy of Theo Hanley)

Celebrating the reopening of St Andrew's church, Leitrim, 30 November 2008. Anne
Corcoran, Tom Corcoran, Suzie Mahony, John Flanagan, Veronica Flanagan, James Grady,
Teresa Flanagan, Mike Nee. (Courtesy of Theo Hanley)

Celebrating the reopening of St Andrew's church, Leitrim, 30 November 2008. Brendan Carty, Gerry Farrell, Sean Callanan, Eileen Callanan, Noel Nevin, Rose Nevin, John Fahy, Eileen Sheehy, John Joe McNabbs, Ambrose Sheehy. (Courtesy of Theo Hanley)

Celebrating the reopening of St Andrew's church, Leitrim, 30 November 2008. Richie Healy, Eddie McKenna, Hilary Molloy, Pat Molloy, Kathleen Healy, Gerry Costello, Mary T. (RIP) and Teresa Dolan, Ina Molloy, Pakie Dolphin, Delia McKenna, Jimmy Leahy, Gretta Costello, Liam Stapleton. (Courtesy of Theo Hanley)

Celebrating the reopening of St Andrew's church, Leitrim, 30 November 2008. Mary Jo Costello, Pat Smyth, Mary Smyth, Maureen Griffin (RIP), guests from New Inn and Gerry Kenny. (Courtesy of Theo Hanley)

Celebrating the reopening of St Andrew's church, Leitrim, 30 November 2008. Sean Flynn, Kathleen Dillon, Pat Dillon, Mary Flynn (RIP), Justin Dillon, Bridie Quinn, Eddie Kenny, Roisín Larkin, Brendan Loughnane, Gavin Treacy. (Courtesy of Theo Hanley)

4

KILTULLAGH, KILLIMORDALY AND ATTYMON

The parish of Kiltullagh lies in what was once the ancient district of Moenmagh, a sub-territory of the O'Kelly principality of the tribe of Hy Many and which was ruled over until the twelfth century by the Hy Mannian families of O'Mullally and O'Naughton, both kin to the O'Kellys. In 1235 the Anglo-Norman Richard de Burgo conquered the province of Connacht and thereafter Moenmagh fell within the de Burgo Lordship of Connacht. In the medieval period, the parish of Kiltullagh contained a rectory and a vicarage. Lying near the northern boundary of Moenmagh, it was known at this time as Cill Tulach Mhaonmuighe to distinguish it from another parish of the same name further north.

After the death of the Earl of Ulster in 1333, his only daughter married Lionel, Duke of Clarence, and with her the de Burgo Lordship of Connacht passed to the Crown. Her uncles, however, revolted and adopted Irish laws and customs with the result that until the sixteenth century, the King's Writ did not run in Connacht.

From the fourteenth century onwards, the Irish employed gallowglasses or Scots mercenary soldiers and paid them in coign, i.e. allotting them certain lands for sustenance, hence the MacSweeney ownership of a townland here. Similar professional men were also paid and thus the O'Dalys were given land for bardic services. They were a Westmeath family. At the Cromwellian settlement, all these properties were forfeited and the lands of Kiltullagh were granted to outsiders but nearly all families were reinstated at the Restoration. The title of the nineteenth-century owners in Kiltullagh springs from this Restoration settlement.

Fr Thomas Dunne and Fr Peter Greaney at the 1942 Jubilee celebrations in Garbally College. (Courtesy of Clonfert Diocesan Archives)

Confirmation in progress in Kiltullagh Church. (Courtesy of Clonfert Diocesan Archives)

Fr Thomas Dunne PP and Revd Prof Tom Fahy outside the parochial house in Kiltullagh.
Fr Dunne was born in Killeenadeema on 2 April 1876 to Peter and Margaret (*née* Hughes)
and was educated at Esker Diocesan College, St Brendan's, Rus-in-Urbe and the Irish College,
Paris. Ordained alongside John Dignan and P.J. Nagle on 6 September 1903, theirs were the
first ordinations to take place at St Brendan's Cathedral, Loughrea. At the time of his death
on 10 November 1967, he was the last surviving student of both Esker and St Brendan's.
CC Kilrickle 1903–05, Ballymacward 1905–06, Eyrecourt 1906–10, Ballinasloe 1910–14,
Portumna 1914–15, CA Loughrea 1915–19. An ardent nationalist in his younger days, he
helped spread the Sinn Féin movement in south-east Galway and acted as a judge on the Sinn
Féin courts. While CA Loughrea, he invited de Valera to the town and entertained him there.
Later, when the British rushed the election of 1920, he attended the SF convention in Athenry
and sponsored the selection of Paddy Hogan. Shortly before leaving Killeenadeema, a bomb
was thrown at the door of his parochial house from a passing police lorry. He succeeded
to Kiltullagh on the death of Fr John Harney, parish priest. Two nephews, Fr Peter Dunne
(1915–2004) and Fr Michael CM, also became priests. Msgr Tom Fahy (1887–1973) was a
native of Gloves, Athenry and was Professor of Ancient Classics for thirty-one years at Galway
University. An ardent republican, he conveyed the news of the disbandment of the Volunteers
to Liam Mellows in 1916 at Ardrahan and later penned Mellows' speech for the 1918 election
when the latter stood in Meath. (Courtesy of Clonfert Diocesan Archives)

St Patrick's Monastery church, Esker 1943. (Courtesy of Clonfert Diocesan Archives)

The beautifully stencilled interior of St Patrick's Monastery Church, Esker 1943. (Courtesy of Clonfert Diocesan Archives)

The O'Connors were there from the seventeenth century as tenant farmers or retainers of one of the landowning families. They are first met by name in the *Tithe Applotment Books* of 1826 which feature at least thirteen landholders or households of the name. Raford townland was the landlord's (O'Daly) demesne but the adjoining townland of Knockatogher had two of the name of O'Connor.

The O'Daly Family

The O'Daly family claimed descent from Nial of the Nine Hostages. One Dermot O'Daly was living at Killymore, County Galway, in 1578. One of his grandsons, also Dermot, was commander at the castle of Claregalway in 1642. Yet another married a D'arcy who was a descendant of the Red Earl. He lived at Karnakelly and was a Privy Councillor to James II. He was also instrumental in having Galway surrender to the forces of William of Orange after the Battle of Aughrim in 1691. A brother, James Daly, lived at Raford which was the seat of the family until the twentieth century. James Daly was succeeded by his grandson Denis who married Lady Anne de Burgo, a descendant of the Earl of Clanricarde.

Fr John W. Clarke (1893–1937) CC Attymon. A native of Redmounthill, Eyrecourt, he was an uncle of Sr Sarah Clarke who worked on behalf of the Birmingham Six and the Guildford Four. While on a sick call in a heavy downpour, he was soaked to the skin and contracted pneumonia. A fortnight later, with his parish priest by his bedside, he died. He was the last priest of the diocese to be educated at the Irish College, Paris and while CC Woodford and Looscaun, oversaw the building of Looscaun parochial house. (Courtesy of Clonfert Diocesan Archives)

Killimordaly

Killimordaly is said to derive from a hermit or thirteenth-century Irish saint, Iomar, a contemporary of St Kerrill of Clonkeenkerrill and of St Conall of Kilconnell. O'Donovan equates the name with a female Irish saint Aobhar, though this is unlikely. The Christian name Iomar was relatively common in Connaught, e.g. Iomar O'Ruadhan, Bishop of Killala and the

Annals of Connaught mention Iomar O'Beirn. The Daly's of Lorrha, in the first two decades of the seventeenth century, established their senior branch and foremost residence at Killimor Castle. As lay patrons and benefactors of the parish they caused the present church to be built. The Daly's of Killimor remained Catholic until the last of them, Anne who was daughter of Darby Daly, married a Protestant clergyman, Revd Nicholas Devereaux of Wexford, in around 1805.

Confirmandi and Fr Dunne, 27 May 1943. (Courtesy of Clonfert Diocesan Archives)

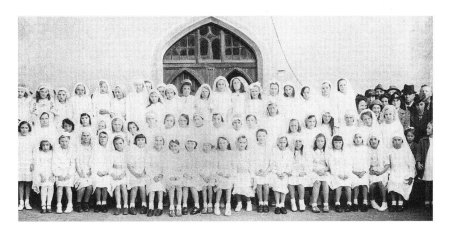

Confirmandi, 27 May 1943. (Courtesy of Clonfert Diocesan Archives)

Confirmation in progress, Kiltullagh Church, 27 May 1943. (Courtesy of Clonfert Diocese)

Curate's residence, Attymon. (Courtesy of Clonfert Diocese)

The present nave of Killmordaly church was added around 1855–1860. The names of the tradesmen involved in the construction are preserved and included John Mitchell of Knockroe West, Jimmy White of Knockroe East (both were masons), with Patch Burke of Gortakeerin (carpenter) whose wife was Hardy of Clonsheecahill. It was Burke who designed the form of erection of the arched style where nave and transept meet.

Esker

The parish has played an important role in the story of the diocesan college. In 1847 Fr Peter Smith OP established a residential school there, but it was short lived. The Rt Hon. Anthony Richard Blake, who was the first Catholic since the Reformation to attain high office under the Crown, was on the Commissioners of National Education and was a co-founder of the Carlisle and Blake Scholarship. He had been a pastman of the old Academy of Loughrea. This had been founded by Bishop Thomas Coen in 1841 but age and infirmity prevented the venerable prelate from putting it on a firm financial footing and it closed. Blake's nephew, Fr Anthony Blake (1815–1898), was a student/boarder at Esker and was its prior when it was established as a diocesan seminary. The Dominican friars, driven from their Athenry Convent by the Reformation, had sought refuge in Esker and after 1704 some became engaged in parochial work. Bishop Thomas Costello was laudatory of them in a report to Rome in 1797, writing: 'The house of Friars Preachers at Esker deserves special praise because I am in the habit of carrying oils there without any cost to myself or the ordinards.'

From 1836, there was quite an enterprise functioning in the place, including a school of 600 children (of whom fifty were fed), a private school and a school where trades were taught. These were all at primary level. Fr Peter Smith, Prior, was the main driving force behind this effort. A more ambitious programme was the establishment of St Dominic's College on 4 August 1847 to provide higher education for better-off Catholics. The curriculum included a literary and classical course and a science course with a bias towards agriculture. Alas, Fr Smith had overreached himself and though it attracted some pupils from Dublin, it closed in 1857. The Famine, the Encumbered Estates Act (a nineteenth-century version of NAMA), the lack of accessibility to Esker and the poor local soil all contributed to its demise. Despite this failure, the Dominicans remained in Esker until 1893; a fire in 1889, however, had all but destroyed the place and in July 1893, the governors of the diocesan college met there and decided to lease the building. Msgr James Madden loaned the diocese £1,000 for the project of restoration. A diocesan collection yielded £473, which with £200 from the Lenten collection and £500 of Msgr Madden's loan became the seed money. Esker College became St Joseph's and Fr John Callanan was the first Rector. Fr Bernard Bowes was the dean of discipline and professor of Latin and Fr Jerome Houlihan, on loan from Killaloe, taught there from 1897 to 1899. The average complement of boarders was thirty-two and thus it remained for the eight years that the college was in Esker. Despite the existence of a college farm, there was a problem in collecting fees and sometimes the shortfall hit the college professors' table. In 1899, eggs were substituted for rashers and luxuries such as coffee, relishes and tinned salmon were discontinued.

In January 1896, the governors fixed the college calendar with festivals to be celebrated. These were St Matthew's Day/Prize Day, St Joseph's Day/High Mass and athletics and St Brendan's Day/Excursion Day. Bishop John Healy often joined the boys on these days to give them the benefit of his historical knowledge. The college continued at Esker until 1901 when a lease was taken of the old Connacht Missionary College in the townland of Portnick, Ballinasloe, known locally as the Pines. With £5,000 from the Redemptorist Order for the old college of Esker, Dr Healy transferred his students to an urban setting.

Kiltullagh National School exterior, children in foreground. (Courtesy of Clonfert Diocese)

Attymon National School. Dr Dignan quizzes children on catechesis, with Fr Thomas Dunne PP (right) and Fr John Hawkins CC. (Courtesy of Clonfert Diocese)

Attymon National School interior. (Courtesy of Clonfert Diocese)

5

CAPPATAGLE AND KILRICKLE

Killalaghton

Cappatagle, fondly referred to by many as 'Cappy', abounds in *béaloideas*. Nothing is known of St Alaghton whom O'Donovan claims gave his name to the only cemetery that serves Cappatagle and there is no name even remotely

Killalaghton orchestra in 1941. Back row, from left to right: Stephen Donohoe, Dan Treacy, Johnny Hynes. Front row: Bridie Donohoe, Annie Fahy, Teresa Glynn, Kitty Kilgannon, Kathleen Manning. (Courtesy of Clonfert Diocesan Archives)

Stephen Donohoe in an unknown role with unidentified front-and-back of a donkey. Plays
were produced in Killalaghton NS until a hall was built in 1939 as the brainchild of Josie
O'Halloran, NT. A Christmas play is still presented to this day by the local community.
(Courtesy of Clonfert Diocesan Archives)

similar in the seventeenth-century *Martyrology of Donegal*. This cemetery,
however, once held a church dedicated to his memory, the site of which is now
marked only by a tree of venerable age. Twenty yards or so from the tree was a
holy well which, alas, was destroyed when the land was drained. One piece of
lore relates how a woman and her children took flight from the dangers posed
by the Battle of Aughrim and besought shelter from the ruined church and
yet another version places the same situation in Famine times. Being unable
to carry all her children, she left one behind and travelled on her way. Upon
return, she found the child alive and well, having been suckled by a branch
from the tree. An older tradition held that a pot of gold was hidden in the
graveyard and guarded by a snake. On moonlit nights of old, the shadow from
the top of the church pointed out the spot where it lay buried.

The Kilrickle Volunteers. Alas, many are unidentifiable. (Courtesy of Jim Fahy)

Hedge Schools

A product of the Penal Code, hedge schools for Catholics operated in Ireland until the mid-nineteenth century. Josie O'Halloran NT investigated possible locations of these sites in 1939 by drawing on the knowledge of older residents. One was said to be in Lurgan on the left side of the road near the house in which Michael Flaherty resided. Built of clay, each morning the children would bring sods of turf to sit on during the day and the following day would burn them. There were no windows, merely square holes, and the *cóipleabhair* of the day were of slate. The teacher was a Mr Cronin and he lodged with the Loughnane family. Two other similar schools operated at Cappatagle Cross and in Cartron near Larkin's forge.

Devotion, Pisreoga and Food

Within the parish there was huge devotion to St Martin whose feast day falls on 10 November and who reputedly kept fowl and stock free of illness. A local belief claimed he had once banished evil spirits from fowl who were

Cartron House, where Bishop Derry resided and which for a time became home to the diocesan college. (Courtesy of Clonfert Diocesan Archives)

fighting each other. Church tradition holds that he was able to communicate with animals, once lovingly exhorting an infestation of mice to depart from his Dominican monastery.

Hallowe'en night was a source of much trepidation but also of fun and tricks. One game had a saucer containing clay, water and a wedding ring. A person was blindfolded, spun about and a hand put to the water meant emigration, to the ring meant an impending marriage and to the clay meant death. In another game a girl and peeled an apple would drape the skin over the door and the next man who walked in would be her future husband. Inevitably, there were some men who preferred to peek in the window prior to entering rather than leave it to chance. In the late nineteenth century it was customary to have only two meals, breakfast and supper, the former consisting of oaten bread and porridge and the latter of milk and potatoes. Nor were kitchen tables the norm. When potatoes were boiled they were spilled onto a skib on top of the pot in the middle of the floor and all tucked in. A noggin of gruel was then handed round from which each took a mouthful. Meat, fish and vegetables were rarities at the time. Eggs were usually eaten on Easter Sunday, noggins substituting for egg cups. The lack of artificial light meant early nights for all.

Ballydonelan Castle, 1913. Within a short space of time, this fine residence would be reduced to its present ruinous state. An attempt to dynamite down the towers in the late 1920s failed. (Courtesy of Clonfert Diocesan Archives)

Fr Tony Cummins was born 6 September 1906, Killeenadeema and educated at the Pines Diocesan College (the last known surviving student at the time of his death) 1921–1923 and also had the distinction of being the last surviving student to move to the new college headquarters at Garbally Park, matriculating into Maynooth in 1925. Ordained 3 April 1932 (early, on account of the Eucharistic Congress), he was CC Clostoken from April to September of that year and then CC Loughrea 1932–1943, CC Killimor 1943–1956, parish priest of Killeenadeema 1956–1964 and parish priest of Cappatagle 1964–1986. He served as Associate Pastor for a further year before retiring to Árus Vianney in October 1987. He died 20 January 2010, at the age of 103 achieving a nice last distinction of being the oldest surviving priest of Clonfert diocese on record. Bishop Peter Donelan long held that record, reportedly having died aged 100 on 7 May 1778. While his forty-five-year tenure as Bishop of Clonfert is unlikely to be beaten, a closer reading of historical documents puts him at 93. (Courtesy of Theo Hanley)

The Fall of the House of Usher

In the townland of Eastwell are the overgrown remains of the former seat of the local landlords, the Usher's. Descended from Arland Usher who was Sheriff of Dublin from 1460–62 and ancestors of the renowned Archbishop Ussher of Armagh, they possessed an imposing mansion, now completely demolished with the exception of the servants' basement. On two noted occasions the family came into conflict with the Catholic Church. On the first of these, 'old' Usher forbade locals to traverse his land to Mass via an old Mass path. This brought him up against the formidable Fr Colman Galvin PP, who in his younger days as CC Attymon had broken up a ring of *shibíní* in advance of the laying of the railway. It was his wont to charge in with a blackthorn stick held aloft and thrash the terrified patrons about the place and out the door. These lowly drinking taverns usually operated from private dwellings without a licence. Galvin confronted Usher who gave orders for one of his sentries to shoot the priest. The sentry became paralysed on the spot and by evening, Usher had contritely sent for the priest to relieve the poor man from his frozen stance.

The latter incident has become known as the 'Eastwell Marriage Case'. William Arland Usher was one upon whom the teachings of the Church sat lightly and he came to desire Mary Caulfield, a housemaid at Eastwell. Being of a traditional bent, she naturally denied his amorous advances, so much so, that he offered to convert to Catholicism. On 24 April 1910, the two were secretly wed in a bedroom in Eastwell House but, alas, the marriage was doomed to come acropper.

Revd John Dermody

Interred in an unmarked grave in the lower right-hand corner of Killalaghton Cemetery are the mortal remains of Fr John Dermody, locally pronounced as 'Darmody'. A native of Clonkeen, he was born around 1850 and stories of his 'powers' are legion. He was born, say the old people, with a cross on his back made of hair, a portent of his supernatural powers. Others say he had a cruciform birthmark on his right shoulder. A nephew of Fr Ferdinand Whyte (who himself was a priest of the diocese and a native of Corbally Beg in Mullagh), Dermody is said to have often fallen foul of Bishop John Healy. Summoned on one occasion to a meeting attended by the bishop himself and some of the clerical mandarins of the diocese, tempers flared and it is said that Dermody rose to his feet and created from thin air a swarm of wasps which were then deployed directly at Healy and his aides. The terrified clerics took flight from the presbytery and fled down Dunlo Street pursued by the cloud of angry insects. On another occasion he was reputedly called to a house in Bullaun where no less than the Devil himself was appearing and conducted an exorcism in a very novel way, by producing a special whistle and blowing into it three times, which had the effect of sucking 'old Nick' back into the hellish hole from whence he came (Good luck to the person that can unravel that piece of folklore). Fr Dermody died in his sleep in March 1908 in Burke's boarding house of Eyre Street, Galway.

Bishop Patrick Fallon

Few finer sons could the parish claim than Patrick Fallon, the last Bishop of Kilmacduagh and Kilfenora before the union of that diocese with Galway in 1866. Born around 1805 to a small farmer in the townland of Fahy, he was a cousin of John Derry, Bishop of Clonfert. He received his early education at Mr Michael Stafford's classical school in Kilchreest and entered Rhetoric in Maynooth on 13 September 1822 as a student for Kilmacduagh. An older brother Thomas had been ordained for Clonfert in 1810 which would suggest he was born around 1786. Patrick Fallon won prizes for every year he was a clerical student bar one and was ordained in 1829. A fluent speaker of Irish, he built the present church of Kiltartan which was consecrated in 1842.

He saw the full horror of the Great Famine in Kiltartan, noting in a letter to the Chief Secretary in 1846 that out of almost 5,000 souls in his care, only thirty had full employment. He also notes that Ireland was a 'Christian country teeming with abundance of all kinds of eatables except the potato, the wretched staple provision of the worst-fed peasant in Europe or perhaps the world.' His exertions ensured the opening of a food depot in Lisdoonvarna. In 1852, he was elevated to the dignity of Kilmacduagh and Kilfenora following the death of Bishop Edmund Ffrench, though his consecration was delayed by almost a year through the machinations of an anonymous letter writer who claimed he was unsuited to the episcopacy. Fallon was an innovator and installed the Christian Brothers in Ennistymon and in 1857 brought the Mercy Order to Gort, bringing his niece, Sr M. Magdalen Fox from the convent in Tuam to ease the Sisters' transition. From 1860 he began to be dogged by ill-health and his duties began to suffer. While Bishop McEvilly of Galway was avariciously eyeing Fallon's episcopal patch, MacHale of Tuam and Derry of Clonfert were more supportive and gave the ailing prelate every encouragement. By July of 1866, Rome had adjudicated that McEvilly should take charge of Kilmacduagh and Kilfenora and Bishop Fallon withdrew to retirement at the Passionist Monastery, Mount Argus, Dublin. The business leading up to McEvilly's takeover of the two ancient dioceses did much to sour him against MacHale whom he felt had tried to thwart him at every turn. One wonders what role McEvilly's own temperament played. In his *History of the Archdiocese of Tuam*, Dean D'Alton records a none-too-favourable opinion of Archbishop McEvilly's last years as successor of St Jarlath. He writes frankly '... Even old priests were often treated with great asperity, their failings shown up, their past services to the Church and to the Archbishop entirely forgotten ... the Archbishop, who had never been popular, became even more unpopular than ever in extreme old age.'

At Mount Argus, Bishop Fallon lived a humble existence and was admitted to the Passionist Order shortly before he died at the age of 74 on 15 May 1879. He was accorded full honours in death, dressed in his episcopal robes and laid on a catafalque. His brother, Thomas, had died as parish priest Ballinakill in the diocese of Clonfert in 1838 and a grandniece, Mother Dominic Fox, died at the Convent of Mercy, Gort, in 1958. A nephew was Fr Patrick Rushe, a famed Carmelite who wrote 'A Second Thebaid: Being a Popular Account of the Ancient Monasteries in Ireland' and 'Carmel in Ireland'. Nothing now remains of the humble dwelling in Fahy, Cappatagle, where Bishop Patrick Fallon was born.

Raftery and Cappatagle

Anthony Raftery (*c.* 1784–1835) holds the reputation of being a national poet and it is said that he resided for a time in Cappatagle with his common-law wife. Alas, the location of the dwelling is now unknown. While aged only 9, he lost his sight through smallpox and as an adult wandered the country supporting himself on his considerable wits. Imbued with bardic talents, he was a welcome guest in many a village for his poetry and song. While laudatory to the hospitable, he could also turn his ire against those he perceived to be none too generous and writes a damning poem about a wedding in Cappatagle where he obviously felt cheated of his due. The poem is a marathon of imprecations against the people and dwells on faction-fighting and unseemly moral behaviour. One should hasten to add that the people of Cappatagle parish are, contrary to Raftery's jaundiced verses, renowned for their decency and hospitality.

Raftery, who spent a goodly number of years wandering the environs of Loughrea, Athenry, Craughwell and Gort, met his end in a small barn belonging to Darby Cloonan at Craughwell. He was buried at night by the light of a candle held by 9-year old Peter Furey on Christmas Eve. Despite

Msgr Edward Stankard, parish priest of Cappatagle since 1986. (Courtesy of Clonfert Diocesan Archives)

the strong gale that was blowing, the candle was said to have remained lit throughout the burial. The poem runs to almost forty verses and Douglas Hyde believed that it was about a couple who had only potatoes and salt herring for their nuptial breakfast. It was more likely about a typical country wedding. It is reproduced here in its entirety mostly for its entertainment and but also for its historic value. Faction fighting on sacramental occasions and on pattern days continued in the Clonfert diocese well into the nineteenth century with fatalities, according to oral tradition, at Chickenswell in Mullagh parish and at St Grellan's Well in Kilcloony. Given the amount of alcohol imbibed on these occasions, the true figure must be much higher.

The poem is reproduced *as Béarla* for the benefit of readers *gan Gaeilge*. Local lore holds that the wedding festivities occurred in the townland of Slehane.

The Big Rill Wedding

An tSl'leachan Mór was host to a feast,
And many say it lasted a week,
A guinea it cost for music sweet,
Five pounds and more to fee the priest,

The juice of the barley there was drawn,
Ale and porter and whiskey too,
'Twas like Tara's Halls, I'm telling you,
When they used to drink from dusk to dawn,

It's there you'd see the mighty crown,
Plenty of lads and nice young girls,
What full-blooded man wouldn't follow them down,
And they like a show when they passed through the town?

There was food and drink for great and small,
And no call for homespun coats at all,
But cambric fine and dresses bright,
And high cockaded for to dazzle your sight,

There was many a frolicsome, winsome lass,
In the latest fashion, let it be said,
If her match was made you'd not let it pass,
To chat her up on the edge of a bed,

Dining tables and matching clouts,
In a row were all laid out,
Dishes bright and plates of pewter,
And sharp-edged knives to meat to carve,

Skewers were produced and the fire was lit,
So that Maura Kane would turn the spit,
Teapots, tureens, china and delf,
Ware that was speckled and white from the shelf,

Most of seven sorts were served at table,
Dressed and prepared before the priest,
Pork and beef and roasted mutton,
Turkey, goose, hen and pullet,

Water partridge on plates was garnished,
Can you name a bird that wasn't there,
Blackbird, plover, woodcock and lark,
Curlew, snipe and ducks from the park,

At party-time, when seated together,
Dressed fish to eat is a wholesome treat,
Trout and salmon, cod if you can,
Maiden ray, red gunnet! That's your man!

Turbot was served as a starter dish,
Followed by ling, bream, plaice and wrasse,
Haddock, mackerel and herrings fresh,
And what would you say to a nice Pollock dish?

But after all that the table's still lacking,
Till we plunder the fruits of the shore and the strand,
Crabs, lobsters, oysters and small shrimps as well,
But you won't get a turtle in its shell,

One and twenty were the dishes, a man and a hundred to serve them up,
But to Mary Loftus, that flower of beauty, without hesitation we raised a cup,
For she it was whose diligent duty,
Was to garnish the dishes from which we sup,

Wedding cakes appeared before us and we sitting down to dine,
And the finest of white bread, crackling and wine,
But the luck of the day well grace the young couple when all's said and done,
For to them, no gainsaying, the profit will come.

Each guest drank a jar from a big foaming tankard,
For the groom is a man of no niggardly purse,

From brandy and punch in glasses o'erflowing,
Full many a vagrant lay stretched on the turf,

Rum and Madeira in tin cans were jumping,
While women all dolled up their Negus were nursing,
And – unless I've been lied to – the following day,
A hundred of them were in a bad way,

The tables were stacked up, the house swept and sprinkled,
There were plenty of seats around the wall,
The music then started, the dancing as well,
Ah, 'twas grand to be there, I can truthfully tell,

With all of the fun you'd find fault, I don't think,
Till the tramps went clean crazy by sheer dint of drink,
And from far Bohermore no bush or ditch,
Was free from the sound of the blows of the stick,

Aged spinsters lay scuttered and sprawled by the ditches,
And I'm sure and certain that they soiled their breeches,
'Twas an awful mistake, now let it be said,
That I missed all the sport and I in my bed,

That very evening you'd see together,
All dressed up, nine hundred beggars,
From Carney's River and Oole O'Malley,
From Oughterard and Connemara,

A letter there was that came through the mail –
Went all round Ireland, so runs the tale,
And each rakish tramp who heard the story,
Packed his gear and stick and prepared for glory,

A nine-foot pole both strong and straight,
A ring on the top and spike fixed tight,
A beggar's wallet, a strap and a bag,
A stout leather belt with its buckle bright,

Along they came from every quarter,
From Droheda and I from Galway,
The Ahascragh road was thronged entirely,
Slieve Aughty's slope was another highway,

There wasn't a hut, a cow-shed or hole,
Where you wouldn't hear roars and you going the road,
Here Paddy Long was a major villain,
And big McGann. Would you like to kill 'em,

A man who was present said to me,
That the tramps were reciting the Rosary,
'Up you get and don't hang back,
Grab hold of your weapon, there's skulls to crack!'

No fence or hedge from Cloch na pairce,
To Cappatagle that wasn't levelled,
And devil a rick, stack or gap by the road,
Where you wouldn't see children, women and beggars,

They formed ranks each other facing,
And then prepared to offer battle,
Cath na bPunann you'd sooner settle,
Than separate them 'fore dawn was breaking,

There were pitchers, kettles, bags and knapsacks,
Flung about outside the village,
There were wounded heads and noses bleeding,
And every thug his stick was wielding,

'Twas in earnest the battle started,
And heads and ears and hair were parted,
When the crown collected and began to fight,
You'd best be gone if you valued your life,

Manus Mor, long ago a hero,
Burned Tara's Halls like an Irish Nero,
Now a hundred like him in this affray,
Wouldn't stand their ground, that's what I say,

Big strong Earcail of the speckled shield,
Who wreaked destruction beside the coast,
The ancient Fianna, that mighty host,
Couldn't compel the thugs to yield,

Conlach, Ardan, Ainle and Naoise,
Who levied taxes in time long past,
Goll MacMorna, An Dearg Mór,
And Taile MacTreoin to complete the cast,

The Siege of Troy – ten years it lasted –
Was a time when countless lives were blasted,
But there's never a man that was marked or made,
Could tell how many the thugs left dead,

Cnoc an Air of notorious fame,
The site, we know, of a deadly game,
But the man who survived wouldn't give rattle,
To hear of Clontarf as a famous battle,

The dead were counted, a thousand and twenty,
On the field of glory and wounded were plenty,
And as many more were smothered and drowned,
Tunning down Corr na Coirce, the inquest found,

On the following day you couldn't fail,
To hear woman and children wail,
They cried to heaven their piteous lack,
Of a man amongst them to carry a pack,

That very day was a list drawn up,
Of men who were fit that gang to stop,
A crown who wandered the country aimless,
And for chasing skirts and fights were famous,

A row there was in this fair land,
Which scattered the beggars out of hand,
But I as the man who made the poem,
And for reward sent payless home,

Now this wasn't the way Eoin's wedding ended,
And while I live I'll sure defend it,
But the revelries done, it must be said,
I had to go thirsty home to bed.

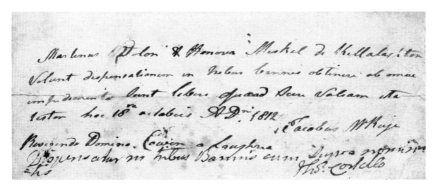

Simpler days … copy of a marriage dispensation signed by Fr James McKeige PP and Bishop Thomas Costello in 1812. (Courtesy of Clonfert Diocesan Archives)

Revd John Kenny O'Neill

Of all the clergy who have served the parish the most vividly recalled is Fr John Kenny O'Neill. Older people remember the timely wit, the story of the bus that broke down because it deliberately failed to stop to bring him to Kilrickle. There was, however, more to J.K. O'Neill than that. A native of Ballymacward, he was a contemporary at the old diocesan college, Esker, of the future Bishop John Dignan. Ordained at St Patrick's College, Carlow, in 1904 he served in curacies in Eyrecourt and Looscaun before enlisting as a Chaplain to the Forces in response to Bishop Gilmartin's appeal to clergy to do the heroic

An iconic photograph showing the SS *Aragon* sinking beneath the waves of the Mediterranean. To the right of the stricken ship is the brow of the trawler which rescued Fr O'Neill. (Clonfert Diocesan Archives)

thing. It has long been the story that he was, at different times, a passenger onboard two troop carriers that were sunk by the enemy. He was, in fact, on board the SS *Aragon* when it was sunk and within minutes of being rescued by a trawler, witnessed the sinking of a destroyer that had just rescued troops that had also been aboard the *Aragon*. Thus, it is likely that the two events, though entirely separate, became conflated in people's memory over time. He describes precisely what happened in a letter to his then superior, Bishop Thomas Gilmartin and which was dated 3 January 1918. O'Neill had sailed aboard the *Aragon* which was a former sea-liner and carried in total 2,500 souls, most of whom were soldiers bound for the battles raging around Palestine. His description of the event is thrilling, though modest, and it is notable that he does not attribute any heroics to himself. He writes:

On Sunday 30th December, I said the 9.30 and 10.15 Masses. I packed up and went to my cabin about 10.45 a.m. I had just begun my breakfast when the great crisis came. Bang! A torpedo had found us and every man to his station! I must say at once that I could not exaggerate the glorious behaviour of everyone on board. The scene was superb and was I am told up to the highest standard of naval behaviour. I begin with the Sisters. The men lined up and not a man moved until all the sisters were away in their boats. Then the men calmly entered the boats allotted them. I was on the poop and when the water came over I and all unattached officers took a good 'header' into the sea. I could swim so instead of going for a raft I struck and for a trawler and came alongside quite fresh. Then the trouble began. I could not climb the rope and was getting exhausted when a sailor gallantly swam to my assistance and firmly leashed me with the rope. I was then hauled on board and a sister gave me brandy as I was in a state of partial collapse. I was quite revived in a few minutes. When we came ashore everybody was very kind to us. I shall not forget all the kindness.

Fr O'Neill avoids mentioning the more harrowing details which must have replayed in his mind on many an occasion. The torpedo had struck the *Aragon* in its oil bunkers with the consequence that many of the men who jumped into the sea from the stricken ship were coated in oil. They had just stripped off their oily garments when rescued by the destroyer HMS *Attack* when that too was torpedoed and almost blown in two so that many were completely naked when thrown back into the oily waters. In all, 610 men died on that occasion including the captain of the *Aragon*, F.T. Bateman. While a Chaplain to the Forces, O'Neill's influence on an aristocratic lady serving as a war-nurse was such that she eventually became a nun in the Carmelite convent in Jerusalem. They corresponded with each other up until her death, just a few months before Fr O'Neill himself died.

As Fr Joseph Fahy's health began to decline, Fr John became CA of Cappatagle parish in 1924 and succeeded the former on his death in 1928. Confessions were always well attended in Cappy church as O'Neill was wont to give general absolution to his flock (blithely oblivious to the fact that faculties to do so had been formally withdrawn from former War-Chaplains by the Holy See in 1919). Tall and powerfully built, he was a skilful horseman in his prime and a thinker too. From time to time he would reflect on the incongruity of non-Gaelic inscriptions on headstones at a time when the language was still spoken. As age advanced upon him, it became necessary that he receive full-time nursing care in Golden, Co Tipperary. Run by nuns, the home where he stayed had been appropriately bequeathed by a general in the British army, Sir William Butler. Butler had penned *The Great Lone Land* (1872), a biography of General Gordon

Dr Dignan and Fr O'Neill with the cemetery committee in Kilrickle. (Courtesy of Clonfert Diocesan Archives)

With the Sphinx as background, Fr O'Neill on a camel (centre) flanked by army officers and locals. (Courtesy of Clonfert Diocesan Archives)

Fr John Kenny O'Neill in military
chaplain's uniform, c. 1916.
(Courtesy of May Roche)

Taken by Fr O'Neill in February 1915,
an interior view of the Jesuit church
reputedly built on the site where the
Holy Family rested during the Flight
to Egypt. (Clonfert Diocesan Archives).

Horseman ride by ... a young Fr O'Neill
astride his mount. (Courtesy of Clonfert
Diocesan Archives)

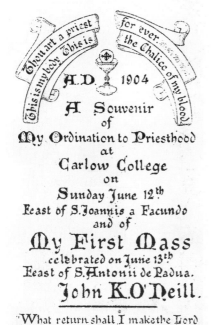

The cardeen ... at ordination a priest usually
produces a small prayer card to commemorate
the occasion. This one was for Fr O'Neill's
ordination. (Courtesy of May Roche)

of Khartoum. Fr John read Mass for the last time on the feast of St Don Bosco, the last day of January. Though advised that morning to rest, he would have none of it, replying 'Do you think I'd fail Don Bosco?' Four days later he died. On 6 February 1964, his Requiem Mass was celebrated by his nephew Msgr Brendan O'Neill, Chancellor of the diocese of Lancaster in England and a noted prison chaplain at Preston. Msgr Brendan's father had a noted career, being Chief Constable in Preston, Lancashire. Another nephew, Canon Desmond O'Neill, acted as deacon.

The people of Cappatagle remember now the 'character', the celebrations at Michaelmas (the feastday of the parish) and the banter in Kilrickle. But who is left to recall the shy young priest from Ballymacward who bravely stepped forward into the savage darkness of a most awful world conflict?

The inscrutable Sphinx ... taken by Fr O'Neill. (Courtesy of Clonfert Diocesan Archives)

6

CARRABANE

There are a few versions of the ecclesiastical title of this parish. The oldest known is Kilconickney, Kilconieran and Lickerrig United, though Fr John Macklin, who built Clostoken church, styled himself PP Lickerrig. In the *1818 Laity's Directory*, the parish priest is designated Carrowbane. Thus, the parish may be fairly referred to as Carrabane as there is a historical precedent.

After the church at Kilconickney fell into a state of ruin, the next known place of worship was in the area called Chapelfield within the Dunsandle Demesne and in the townland of Carrabane which itself is derived from the 'white quarter'. This chapel was used until Fr Macklin had Clostoken church erected in 1842. The old church of Kilconieran was plain and rectangular and was built by Revd Hugh Colgan who was at one time considered a possible successor to Bishop Thomas Coen of Clonfert. In 1833 he gave the site for Lickerrig school which was built with £150 from the Education Commissioners and £80 raised locally. Prior to 1812, a thatched house near a hillock called Cnoc na Séipéal served as both school and chapel. In 1931, an elderly resident claimed that the Irish language had died out locally after the establishment of the National Schools due to the harsh punishment meted out to those who dared to speak it. In September 1961, the new church of Kilconieran was consecrated with the sermon preached by Fr Thomas Keyes and the Mass celebrated by a native of Kilconieran, Fr Patrick Fallon.

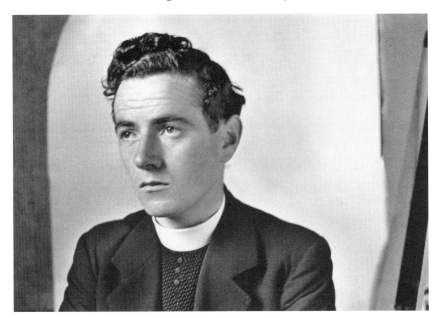

Fr William Naughton (1916–2002) just after ordination in 1941. His uncle Thomas was parish priest of Ballymacward and his father William was principal at Creagh National School, Ballinasloe. He spent his early years of ministry in Los Angeles as there were too many clergy in Clonfert diocese. (Courtesy of Clonfert Diocesan Archives)

Fr Gilbert Egan PP in the doorway of Dunsandle Tower House. (Courtesy of Clonfert Diocesan Archives)

Fr Gilbert Egan as a schoolboy at the Pines Diocesan College, *c.* 1910. Born 13 December 1892 to John and Anne (*née* Dempsey) in Woodford, he was educated first at St John's National School, Woodford and the Pines Diocesan College. Later Fr Peter Greaney, when recalling his school years of 1910–1913 at the Pines, would say of him: 'Gilby Egan was … senior class. He was a thin boy with a long blue face. Gilby had an extra box in the room … and he used to be smoking Woodbines there. No young boy had permission to go in there. "Wooden foot" was his nickname, and everyone used say that he had a real wooden foot under him. You wouldn't know from looking at Gilby what thoughts used to go around in his head. He had a secretive face.' He trained at the Irish College in Rome, where he was ordained in 1917. On loan to Dunkeld

diocese, Scotland 1917–1920, serving at St Joseph's parish, Dundee, on his return he taught English at St Joseph's Diocesan College, Garbally Park, Ballinasloe 1920–1925. Very Revd Dr Kevin Egan (1911–2001), who was a student there at the time, later recalled his departure: 'The first to leave was Fr Egan. He had been teaching English and was referred to us as "Dido", which might denote a classical connection but I think it derived from English literature: "On such a night stood Dido with a willow in her hand upon the wild sea banks and waved her love to come again to Carthage." There was no logic in the bestowal of nicknames.' He was CC Gurteen 1925–1926, Kilrickle 1926–1929, CC Eyrecourt 1929–1939, before finally moving to Carrabane on Fr Pat O'Farrell's death. He had begun preparations to build a new church at Kilconieran when he died 2 January 1956. (Courtesy of Marie O'Carra)

Post-confirmation gathering outside Holy Family Church, Clostoken, 13 May 1943. (Courtesy of Clonfert Diocesan Archives)

Confirmation in progress in Clostoken, 13 May 1943. (Courtesy of Clonfert Diocesan Archives)

Holy Wells

Near St Columbkille's triple well, in the townland of Boherduff, were old foundation stones which local lore said marked the spot where Columbkille once lived. In a field nearby was St Colman's Well which consisted of two round hollows in a big stone. St Fallon's Well was near the ruin of a leper hospital which was a sub-branch of a similar building in Loughrea. Kelly's Well was in the townland of Lackafinna and at one time these wells were the focal point of patterns, all of which have now died out. A vague tradition holds that the townland of Kilasbuig Moylan took its name from a Bishop Moylan, slain in battle and interred therein but no other details are known. Cnocán a Pobail or the little hill of the congregation is in Moyode townland and was the location of Masses when public worship was proscribed by the Penal Code.

Castles

The parish abounds with the remains of Anglo-Norman tower-houses and fine manors, including Rathruddy, Lackafinna, Dunsandle and St Cleran's. The stones of Clonoo castle went into the building of Dalyston House in Leitrim parish and in Clonoo Castle it was that Bishop Ambrose Madden hid in the dangerous days of the Penal Code. Moyode castle was built in 1820 by Mr Pearse and was burned down in 1922 by republicans. These Persse's set up a Protestant school at Slieveroe, not far from the gate of Moyode but only a few attended. One girl who converted to Protestantism became a servant at Wade's in Ballinasloe. St Cleran's was occupied by film director John Huston from the 1950s until 1973 and he was well liked by locals. Built in 1784 by the Burke family, it was the birthplace of Robert O'Hara Burke who later became an explorer and the first man to cross Australia from south to north. He was to perish, however, on an expedition in 1861. St Cleran's was bought in 1997 by the American chat-show host Merv Griffin but has recently changed ownership.

Dunsandle Tower House.
(Courtesy of Clonfert
Diocesan Archives)

Schooling

It was at Clostoken that Michael Stafford held his classical school. Reference to him is found in Msgr Jerome Fahey's *History and Antiquities of the Diocese of Kilmacduagh*. Fahey states that Bishop Patrick Fallon, who was a native of Fahy townland in Cappatagle, was educated by Stafford at Kilchreest. We also know that he educated a number of other future priests of Clonfert so his reputation was obviously high. While little is known of Stafford's background, it appears he was a native of Nenagh and an ex-soldier who fought in the Napoleonic Wars. He had the benefit of studying in the libraries and museums on the Continent which gave him a distinct edge over other hedge school masters. Old people in Clonoo, as far back as the 1930s, could recall some who were educated by him speaking Latin and Greek with a fair degree of fluency. Fahey also claims that Stafford had been an ecclesiastical student. He had a reputation for eccentricity, to which he was entitled, given his colourful life.

General

Up until around 1860 there were some five or six cornmills but only one survived up to the Emergency, with no cottage industries. Baskets were made in great abundance by most people for home uses such as carrying produce

Dr Dignan, Henry Dowd NT, Monica Slattery NT and Fr Egan PP. (Courtesy of Clonfert Diocesan Archives)

and holding turf. The growing of flax was commonplace with spinning, weaving and dyeing widespread. Rush lights dipped in grease were the providers of light up to around 1870 and matches were introduced locally at the same time. Dancing at crossroads and indeed on sandhills was once hugely popular, with music provided by flute and fiddle.

Old Kilconieran Church, deconsecrated since 1961. The building is still extant. (Courtesy of Clonfert Diocesan Archives)

Fr Gilbert Egan PP within the sanctuary of old Kilconieran Church. Dr Dignan seated, right, almost out of view. (Courtesy of Clonfert Diocesan Archives)

Sr Teresa Keogh, a native of Dougrane townland,
Clostoken and Daughter of Charity. (Courtesy of
Eileen Sheehy)

Sr Teresa Keogh on a visit home to Dougrane. (Courtesy of Eileen Sheehy)

7

NEW INN
AND BULLAUN

Following the Anglo-Norman invasion, parishes had rectors and vicars with rectories, a system for the provision of revenues to support religious houses. They involved the tithes of certain lands with the vicars doing pastoral work. *The Ecclesiastical Taxation of Ireland* in 1306 lists the rector of *Buellis* in the deanery of Loughrea. This refers to the Cistercian Abbey of Boyle, established from Mellifont firstly under Bishop Peter O'Mordha who later became Bishop of Clonfert and was drowned in the Shannon in 1171. This rectory later became known as the parish of Grange. The name itself reveals the monastic connection as it refers to the granary supplying the monastery. Post-Reformation, its boundaries remained fixed and later it remained the civil parish upon which were based the census returns of the nineteenth century. When Catholic parishes were joined together in the Penal era due to the paucity of clergy, Grange became united to Bullaun and Killane.

There is evidence that there was a church in Bullaun around 1300 and again for a short period in the sixteenth century under the care of a religious community, but the latter was confiscated. It was dedicated to St Patrick and consequently it was Revd Dr Kevin Egan's suggestion that the present church of Bullaun be similarly dedicated in 1972. Fr Bryan Lorcan, ordained in Killoran in 1679 by Bishop Tadhg Keogh, ministered in a wretched Mass cabin. In 1803 a church was built at New Inn to replace the church of the Penal era which was used up until 1801 and which stood in the hills around 150 yards north-west of the Garda station. The 1803 structure was reconstituted eighty years later by Fr Thomas Head, parish priest. He also built the old parochial house and three schools. The name of New Inn arose due to the siting there of a depot owned by Arthur Guinness which latterly became the site of the police barracks.

Bullaun's Holy Well

This well was located in Ballyeighter near the hill of Carane and attracted great crowds in the month of July when pilgrims came to give thanks and perform penance for sins. During a dry season when the well dried up, it is said that one individual transported water to it from a neighbouring well. She then sold the holy water for a couple of pence per saucepan. Tobar a' Domhnaigh was the focus of a pattern but as time passed faction fights arose and clergy were obliged to suppress the pattern day when a man was killed there around 1850.

Successor and predecessor … Fr Hubert Murray PP and Fr Tom Grady PP. (Courtesy of Clonfert Diocesan Archives)

Fr Thomas Moloney, parish priest of Killeenadeema/Aille and Fr Martin Tuohy, parish priest of New Inn/Bullaun, *c*. 1930. Fr Tuohy (1882–1947) was a native of Looscaun and was ordained in 1906. He was noted for attending to pastoral duties while tearing around the parish on a motorcycle. Fr Moloney preferred the push-cycle, as is evident from the clips on the bottom of his trouser legs. (Courtesy of Clonfert Diocesan Archives)

Dr Dignan and upkeep committee in Killaan Cemetery. (Courtesy of Clonfert Diocesan Archives)

Fr John Kelly, Dr Dignan and upkeep committee in Grange Cemetery. (Courtesy of Clonfert Diocesan Archives)

New Inn Church with bell visible in tree, 1945. It was built in 1882 by Fr Thomas Head PP and replaced an earlier structure erected in 1803, which stood a few hundred yards away. Fr Head was a native of Carhoon, Tynagh and when he died in 1893, was the last surviving priest of Clonfert diocese to have witnessed the horrors of the Great Famine. (Courtesy of Clonfert Diocesan Archives)

Bullaun Church in 1945. It was demolished twenty-five years later to make way for a new church. (Courtesy of Clonfert Diocesan Archives)

Bullaun Church sanctuary, 1945. (Courtesy of Clonfert Diocesan Archives)

The Turoe Stone

First coming to the notice of scholars in 1903, it is one of the finest extant examples of *La Téne* or classical Celtic art. Once standing near the Rath of Feerwore, it was moved in the nineteenth century to be a garden ornament

The Turoe Stone. (Courtesy of Theo Hanley)

for Turoe House, which now plays host to a popular pet farm. Scholars date it to around 300 years prior to the Christian Era. A granite boulder measuring 1.68 metres in height, it is in the shape of a domed cylinder, with a step-like pattern around its middle. The upper portion is covered with various motifs including stylised animal heads. Some have likened it to the phallus and regard it as an ancient fertility symbol while others propose that it represents the four corners of the earth.

Schooling

Mr Melody and Mr Sheridan taught school at the old chapel using the *Reading Made Easy* and *Double Spelling Book* and a night school was conducted by Mr Patsy Power at Ballyfa. Johnny Rowan had a day-and-night school at Cartron (now Lecarrowshruhaun) and was occasionally assisted by his wife. A teacher named Manannan (*sic*) lived at Crossmacrin and had a school of sorts there. Miss Jackson travelled about to teach English while Johnny Kelly taught catechism after Mass. John Higgins, Woodlawn, taught catechism in English. A Mr Foreman had a soup school at Woodlawn and some Catholics attended. Lady Ashtown sponsored items like blankets to give to the poorer families who attended and a Christmas party was held for them at Woodlawn. Similar proselytysing shindigs took place at Buckhill and were organised by a Mrs Villiers.

Woodlawn National School. (Courtesy of Clonfert Diocesan Archives)

Bullaun National School. (Courtesy of Clonfert Diocesan Archives)

Dr Dignan examines catechesis, Bullaun National School, 1945. (Courtesy of Clonfert Diocesan Archives)

Dr Dignan in Woodlawn National School. (Courtesy of Clonfert Diocesan Archives)

Recreation

In 1931 Fr Martin Tuohy PP, wrote with some prescience to Bishop Dignan that 'The modern immoral dances have not yet come to us from the towns, but as there is no hall or encouragement presently here, the young people will seek amusement in the towns.' More banal pastimes were hurling and football while wrestling became obsolete at the start of the twentieth century. Coursing and hunting were prevalent until around 1920 as was bird-catching via birdnets and cradles.

Pisreoga

Weddings were the source of much superstition and it was held that the bride or bridegroom who exited the church first after the ceremony would be the first to die. It was also considered luckier to meet a man as they exited the church rather than a woman. Cures were of great topicality, with the milk of an ass a sovereign remedy for chin-cough, or indeed another means of curing the same complaint was to travel until one met a man on a white horse. To enter a house for a coal to light a pipe and depart with the coal would take the luck out of the house and meeting a weasel on a journey boded ill. Cranes portended bad weather if flying inland and if one flew over the head of a pregnant woman, it was believed that death would befall either mother or child. A wisp in a hen's tail also indicated a death in the family. If the tongs fell into the fire a stranger would soon arrive and on visiting a sick person one would spit upon them or in their general direction (hygiene was generally a casualty of a goodly number of customs).

The Butter and the Corpse

A curious little ghost story concerns a field called Coolacally, situated on the western edge of Turoe Wood. Here lived a young man called Seán Healy with his mother and with whom he was ever at loggerheads. One night, while in his cups, he lost his temper and struck her a blow from which, to use the parlance of the nineteenth-century obituarists, she fell down quite dead. Healy was seized with terror and spotting a firkin or butter cask, decided to bury the old woman expeditiously. Hoisting the firkin on his back he set off to Toolobane graveyard but when he reached the field now called Coolacally, he met a neighbour called Tomás Higgiston with another firkin on his back, in which was secreted butter that he had stolen at Toolobane. They sat to chat and draw their breaths and when about to set out again, took up the wrong casks. Healy took the butter to the graveyard and buried it but Higgiston began to notice blood seeping from the firkin and in his terror buried it on the spot. Both men, whenever passing this spot, were chased by the ghost of the old woman and locally the place became known as Coolacally or 'the old hag's corner'.

The Phillips Family

One of the notable families, now gone from this district, were the Phillips. George Phillips, who died in 1926, aged 95, was a nephew of Fr John O'Connor parish priest Aughrim and the last priest to be tried under the old Penal laws for contracting a marriage between a Catholic and a Protestant. George's mother had died in 1847 of Famine fever while tending to starving neighbours and he was left alone at the age of 16 to raise his young siblings. Later, two of his daughters would become nuns and a son, Augustine, became a Carmelite priest.

Colleagues relaxing in mufti … Fr Hycie O'Callaghan, Hubert Murray and Pat Abberton, on holidays in Normandy, c. 1950. (Courtesy of Clonfert Diocesan Archives)

New Inn/Bullaun Pioneer Council at a function in Hayden's Hotel, December 1974.
Back row, from left to right: Michael Mullen (RIP), John Ryan (RIP), Fr Hubert Murray PP (RIP), Frank Corcoran, Ann Mullen (RIP), Seamus Doyle, (Senator) Michael Mullins, Fr Martin McNamara. Front row: Esther Corcoran, Anne O'Beirn, Maureen Doyle.
(Courtesy of Clonfert Diocesan Archives)

Sr Anne McGuinness, a native of New Inn and Columban Sister. Sr Anne has another sister in the Columban Order and her brother, Michael, is a priest. (Courtesy of Eileen Sheehy)

8

KILLEENADEEMA AND AILLE

Extending from Loughrea to the boundary of County Clare, its name according to the antiquarian scholar John O'Donovan signifies the 'church of St Dima', though the parish has been under the patronage of St Dympna since the early nineteenth century. A holy well near the old church in Killeenadeema East

A soft day, thank God … parishioners greet Dr Dignan and Fr Bill O'Mahony PP outside St Dympna's church, Killeenadeema after confirmations, 25 May 1943. (Courtesy of Clonfert Diocesan Archives)

Same, different view. (Courtesy of Clonfert Diocesan Archives)

Confirmation in progress, Killeenadeema, 25 May 1943. Clergy on sanctuary: Revd
Dr John O'Connor, Revd Tony Cummins, Revd Bill O'Mahony. (Courtesy of Clonfert
Diocesan Archives)

Full group of confirmandi outside St Dympna's church, Killeenadeema, 25 May 1943.
(Courtesy of Clonfert Diocesan Archives)

was not in use in O'Donovan's time, except by very old residents whom he says were scoffed at by some locals. Older people told him that the well was the focus of a pattern up to around 1800, at the time of year 'when people used to be in a hurry sowing the potatoes'. O'Donovan also states that the mountainous territory of Sliabh Echtghe begins in the townland of Coppanagh and extends to County Clare.

Imposing Sliabh Aughty

The legend runs that Aughty gets its name from Echtghe Nathach, the daughter of Ursothac, son of Tinde, who was one of the Tuatha de Dannan. This tribe were regarded as immortals who were capable of changing shape and ruled Ireland as mythical ancestors of the chieftains and kings of the historic period. Echtghe was fostered by the side of Sith Nanta by Moch Maelgeann. She married Lusca MacRuidí, a royal cup-bearer reputed to have been nursed by a serpent as a child. It was a sound match because of the lands he owned which stretched from Moenmoy and towards the Shannon to the western ocean. He had no wealth but only the land which was the right of his office. She had cattle which needed grazing and after he gave up his grazing rights to her, the mountain became known by her name. Two particular cows were chosen from Echtghe's herds because of their productivity, one being grazed on the north side of the mountain and the other on the south. The story goes that the cow on the north did not yield half of the milk produced by the cow on the south side, though many have disputed this claiming that the north side is more fertile. A proof of this, says the Annals, is the existence of a townland called Derrybrien or 'the grove of quarrel and contention'. Through it runs a river called Abhainn Sa Loigheach or 'the river of the two milch cows'.

The Legend of Sliabh Aughty

An ancient tale relates how the three most learned men of Connacht were named MacLiag, MacCoisi and Fann MacLonan. The people of the time knew them as 'the servant of man, the servant of God and the servant of the Devil', the last so-named because of his vituperative nature. His compositions were calculated to lampoon and degrade the locals while MacCoisi, the servant of God, had a very charitable nature and died whilst on pilgrimage. MacLiag was renowned for his neighbourly disposition.

With MacLonan's death, his tympanist, Illrechtach switched to service for MacLiag and one day he and his new master set out to converse with Brian Boru. Taking the route from Loughrea, they crossed the Aughties and travelled southwards to Clare and Limerick. For refreshment they took sufficient food and twelve vessels of drink for there are twelve aspects on the journey from which great views are to be seen. Upon the hill of *Ceann Crochain*, MacLiag reputedly said, 'Many a hill and lake and dingna [great feature] now lie before us and to know them all were great knowledge.' Illrechtach imprudently remarked 'Were my old master MacLonan here, he would know the Dinnseanchas [topographical lore] of every one of those places.' MacLiag gave Orders for him to be hanged on the spot but the musician appealed to him for a short reprieve and prayed and fasted through the night so that the soul of MacLonan might come to his rescue. MacLonan's ghost appeared early on the morn and said, 'Release the prisoner and I will tell you the history of every dingna here in Aughty.' Thus was Illrechtach's life spared. In grand Gaelic verse, MacLonan enumerated fifty-six places of beauty on the rugged ranges of the mountain, including Ceann Crochain, which took its name from the tale that Crochain, chief of the Tuatha de Danann, was decapitated and his head buried there.

While the poem and the story are what O'Donovan called a 'fabrication', they preserve a list of names of curious places in one of the most beautifully Gaelic forms of folklore to be found in the diocese of Clonfert. With tales such as these, the ancient bard was on his most celebrated form and the ancient poets were thus believed to have the power to summon the ghost of any man from any period of history to consult with them on disputed historical events.

Sonnagh National School. The school closed in the late 1950s. One of its former pupils was Michael Carty who became a TD and Chief Whip in Fianna Fáil. His aunt, Mrs Winifred Murray, had been principal there for many years. (Courtesy of Clonfert Diocesan Archives)

Dr Dignan examining catechesis in Sonnagh National School. A bright spark seeks the bishop's attention while Fr Bill O'Mahony PP looks on. (Courtesy of Clonfert Diocesan Archives)

Sonnagh National School confirmation candidates, 1943. (Courtesy of Clonfert Diocesan Archives)

The former parochial residence, Killeenadeema. (Courtesy of Clonfert Diocesan Archives)

Cllr Pat Hynes, a native of Ballynagreeve, with former Cllr Hugh Loughnane of Shanaglish, 1977. Hugh, who died 16 April 1978, aged 85, was a brother of Pat and Harry Loughnane who were brutally murdered by the Auxiliaries on 26 November 1920. (Courtesy of Cllr Pat Hynes)

Interdict

Killeenadeema has the dubious distinction of having once been placed under interdict, an ecclesiastical censure which in effect is a blanket excommunication. Interdicts take two forms. The first is a personal interdict in which a priest may be forbidden to celebrate the sacraments in a particular district. The second, which applies to an area, is called a local interdict. Though rarely used, it is not quite obsolete and some prelates still regard it as one of the last shots in the spiritual locker when dealing with what they regard as incorrigible behaviour. The town of Adria in Italy was interdicted in 1909 by Pope Pius X following an attack on the local bishop. In that instance, the Pope forbade all liturgical celebrations, sacraments and the ringing of the church bells.

In Clonfert there are two recorded instances of the invocation of interdict, both in the nineteenth century. The cause in the case of Killeenadeema and Kilteskill (it was not united to Aille until after 1858) was the attendance of Catholics at the Bible school which was under the auspices of Lord Clancarty. No person was permitted to dwell on estate land unless they attended but in 1823 Bishop Thomas Coen threatened to excommunicate those who did. In effect, the people found themselves choosing between eviction and excommunication and given their wretched lot, they chose the latter. This was at a time when people did not move as freely as today between parish churches and thus the entire populace of the parish was barred from the sacraments. Eventually, the interdict was lifted and the people were reconciled with the Church.

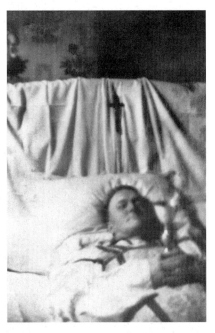

A holy man at rest ... Fr PJ Leahy (1888–1943) laid out in his priestly robes and with chalice in hand. Fr Leahy was a native of Ballynagreeve, son of Michael and Mary (*née* Donnellan) and a hugely popular pastor. Buried in Meelick, a notable number of people have told the writer that they still travel there to pray for his intercession. (Courtesy of Clonfert Diocesan Archives)

Dr Dignan, Fr O'Mahony and cemetery committee at St Mary's church, Aille. (Courtesy of Clonfert Diocesan Archives)

Dr Dignan and Fr O'Mahony with teachers from Aille National School. (Courtesy of Clonfert Diocesan Archives)

Fr Thomas Moloney PP 1931–1942. (Courtesy of Clonfert Diocesan Archives)